PUTTING UNIVERSITIES IN THEIR PLACE

AN EVIDENCE-BASED APPROACH TO UNDERSTANDING THE CONTRIBUTION OF HIGHER EDUCATION TO LOCAL AND REGIONAL DEVELOPMENT

LOUISE KEMPTON, MARIA CONCEIÇÃO REGO,
LUCIR REINALDO ALVES, PAUL VALLANCE,
MAURÍCIO AGUIAR SERRA AND MARK TEWDWR-JONES

Regional Studies Policy Impact Books
Series Editor: Philip R. Tomlinson

RSA Regional Studies
Association

Research Today, Policy Tomorrow

First published 2021
by Taylor & Francis
4 Park Square, Milton Park, Abingdon, Oxon, OX14 4RN

Taylor & Francis Group, an informa business

© 2021 Louise Kempton, Maria Conceição Rego, Lucir Reinaldo Alves,
Paul Vallance, Maurício Aguiar Serra and Mark Tewdwr-Jones

British Library Cataloguing-in-Publication Data
A catalogue record for this book is available from the British Library.

Trademark notice: Product or corporate names may be trademarks or registered trademarks, and are used only for identification and explanation without intent to infringe.

ISBN13: 978-1-032-05566-4 (print)
ISBN13: 978-1-003-19815-4 (e-book)

Typeset in 10.5/13.5 Univers LT Std
by Nova Techset Private Limited, Bengaluru and Chennai, India

Disclaimer: Every effort has been made to contact copyright holders for their permission to reprint material in this book. The publishers would be grateful to hear from any copyright holder who is not here acknowledged and will undertake to rectify any errors or omissions in future editions of this book.

Disclosure statement: No potential conflict of interest was reported by the authors.

CONTENTS

PUTTING UNIVERSITIES IN THEIR PLACE

An evidence-based approach to understanding the contribution of higher education to local and regional development

FOREWORD

Higher education institutions (HEIs) have become important actors in our knowledge-intense economies. An increasing number of universities and colleges have developed strong linkages with stakeholders outside the academic community, with benefits from their research and teaching activities, which generate societal and economic value. Notably, some HEIs have gone even further by developing collaboration within their own ecosystems and networks. These HEIs represent powerhouses of innovations, skills, resilience and sustainability for their own networks.

The Covid-19 pandemic has exacerbated the need for HEIs to interact with their own ecosystems. By disrupting the routine, the health crisis has forced HEIs to develop stronger bonds with their students, academic staff and, most importantly, surrounding communities. Symmetrically, the health crisis has shed light on the capacity of institutions to act as innovation drivers within their ecosystems, and to build resilience by creating new linkages with regional actors.

To unleash the potential of "engagement", higher education policy should move from a space-blind approach to the idea that place-responsiveness is an important feature of a modern HEI. In other words, abandon a one-size-fit-all policy and give actors and stakeholders the possibility to adjust national regulations, incentives and even metrics to the needs and conditions of communities and networks. Through this model, HEIs can generate interactions reflecting both the concepts of "proximity" and "community" without the risk of becoming "localistic".

Undoubtedly, more needs to be done to facilitate the collaboration between HEIs and their ecosystems to ensure that their potential is maximized—and now is the time to act. This publication provides a timely boost to the urgency of generating synergies between higher education and regional development. In the same vein, building on the work of the Organisation for Economic Co-operation and Development's (OECD) Local Economic and Employment Development (LEED) Committee, the "Geography of Higher Education" stands at the core of education, economic and regional development policies, and contributes to creating the impetus for HEIs to build partnerships with their communities and networks. Investing in innovative,

https://doi.org/10.1080/2578711X.2021.1891730

connected and embedded HEIs is one of the highest return investments that we can make to empower students, individuals and communities vis-à-vis the future of work and society.

Raffaele Trapasso
Economist, Centre for Entrepreneurship, SMEs, Cities and Regions, OECD,
Paris, France

https://doi.org/10.1080/2578711X.2021.1891730

ABOUT THE AUTHORS

Louise Kempton is Senior Research Associate at the Centre for Urban and Regional Development Studies (CURDS), Newcastle University, UK.
✉ louise.kempton@newcastle.ac.uk; ⓘ 0000-0002-4684-5565

Maria Conceição Rego is Professor in the Department of Economics and a researcher in the Centre for Advanced Studies in Management and Economics (CEFAGE), University of Évora, Portugal.
✉ mcpr@uevora.pt; ⓘ 0000-0002-1257-412X

Lucir Reinaldo Alves is Professor in the Department of Economics and a researcher in the Centre for Regional Development (NDR), Western Paraná State University, Brazil and a researcher in the Centre of Geographical Studies (CEG) at the University of Lisbon, Portugal.
✉ lucir.alves@unioeste.br; ⓘ 0000-0001-5703-623X

Paul Vallance is a Research Associate in the Centre for Regional Economic and Enterprise Development (CREED), Sheffield University Management School, University of Sheffield, UK.
✉ p.vallance@sheffield.ac.uk; ⓘ 0000-0002-0024-7105

Maurício Aguiar Serra is Professor of Economic Development in the Institute of Economics, University of Campinas, Brazil.
✉ mserra@unicamp.br; ⓘ 0000-0002-5643-425X

Mark Tewdwr-Jones is UCL Bartlett Professor of Cities and Regions, The Bartlett Centre for Advanced Spatial Analysis (CASA), University College London, UK.
✉ m.tewdwr-jones@ucl.ac.uk; ⓘ 0000-0002-8786-6434

https://doi.org/10.1080/2578711X.2021.1891735

EXECUTIVE SUMMARY

The past 50 years have seen a massive expansion in higher education (HE), especially in middle-income countries. There has also been significant growth in student mobility, though this tends to favour higher income countries which enjoy positive net flows at the expense of lower income ones.

University missions evolve over time and in response to external demands. Recent decades have seen a transformation in the role of higher education institutions (HEIs) in regional development. There are mutual benefits, for example, universities get access to new funding streams and regional partners get access to knowledge, innovation and technology. But effective regional partnerships require trust and can often be a time-consuming process. Relationships need to go beyond superficial displays of cooperation through, for example, the signing of high-level agreements such as memoranda of understanding.

The primary value of HE to a region is through enhancing human capital. This can stimulate productivity, entrepreneurship and innovation. However, this presents a challenge for peripheral or lagging regions: graduates are generally highly mobile, with a tendency to migrate to the most high-performing places; the presence of HEIs in a region alone is therefore not sufficient to ensure it will benefit from this uplift in human capital relative to other regions.

Involving universities in regional strategies to develop, support and grow new sectors can mitigate his effect by creating employment and business opportunities for graduates. However, matching HE provision to local needs is a high-risk approach that may have the opposite effect for which it is intended, as HEIs and places can become "locked in" in a spiral of mutual decline.

Some regions may develop strategies based on university research, driving new path creation, while others focus on their role in path adaptation. The former is a high-risk–high-reward strategy that, evidence shows, only succeeds in exceptional cases.

A focus of universities' contribution on the supply side (generating graduates and new knowledge through research) is not sufficient, especially on the periphery. There is also a need to develop the demand-side (absorptive capacity) and translational dimensions of knowledge transfer.

https://doi.org/10.1080/2578711X.2021.1891747
© 2021 Louise Kempton, Maria Conceição Rego, Lucir Reinaldo Alves,
Paul Vallance, Maurício Aguiar Serra and Mark Tewdwr-Jones

This study demonstrates the most significant contribution of universities to regional economies is by supporting the development of regional resilience and adaptive capacity through teaching and research. This requires universities to have engagement and impact strategies that go beyond the direct economic effect of their presence in the local economy.

This presents particular challenges for policymakers in peripheral regions because they need to do more than their counterparts in core regions to develop the demand side and attract and retain skilled people.

Various models of university–region relations for development have had a big impact on shaping policy. However, they have inherent weaknesses, especially in terms of their application in less developed or peripheral regions. In addition, they do not take sufficient account of the diversity of institutional, policy and regional settings.

https://doi.org/10.1080/2578711X.2021.1891747

KEY RECOMMENDATIONS

Regional engagement of higher education institutions (HEIs) depends to a large extent on the role an HEI chooses to assume for itself, which is driven by a range of factors, including internal leadership, institution size, age and history. **Policymakers should consider these factors and their impact when designing strategies to involve HEIs in regional development.**

The model of higher education implicit in many approaches to conceptualizing the role of HEIs in regional engagement is often that of a single, large, "full service" anchor institution with a long history of deep ties to its place, and it is rarely the case in practice. Our research demonstrates that the reality is often characterized by high levels of heterogeneity of higher education configurations between places. **Policymakers should understand this high level of diversity and avoid duplicating "one size fits all" approaches or models of success from other places.**

In places with multiple HEIs, universities may take on different roles in regional development, depending on their individual characteristics and perceived position compared with the other HEIs in the region. **Policymakers should not therefore treat the sector as a homogenous whole, but rather understand the specificities of its component parts and design policies and programmes that play to the strengths and motivations of individual institutions to maximize their contribution.**

We recommend policymakers use *The ORPHIC Framework* so they can work with HEIs in their region to understand and map their various roles and contributions. This will help identify gaps and overlaps, which funding programmes can help address by incentivizing HEIs to play new or enhanced roles in line with regional strategies for development.

The importance of the character of the regional context to the contribution HEIs can make to regional development should not be underestimated. **Policymakers should consider these factors in the design of regional programmes and incentivize HEIs to take part in activities that support the development of resilience and adaptive capacity.**

There is no single blueprint for the role of an HEI in regional development: it will evolve over time in response to external pressures and internal changes. **Policymakers need a flexible framework to**

https://doi.org/10.1080/2578711X.2021.1891748

understand the role and contribution HEIs can make to regional development, which should be regularly reviewed and revised in response to changing circumstances.

Much of the rhetoric on the role of HEIs in regional development is overoptimistic. It ascribes an excessively prominent role for HEIs than evidence would suggest is warranted, and which downplays the significance of the challenges in achieving mutually beneficial outcomes. Ambitious programmes for engaging HEIs in regional development that are not grounded in reality will be at best ineffectual, but may even lead to the widening of disparities between the region and other places. **More modest, but realistic, programmes may prove more effective in the longer term.**

https://doi.org/10.1080/2578711X.2021.1891748

1. INTRODUCTION

Keywords: universities, innovation, economic growth, regions

It is widely acknowledged and accepted that universities[1] are key repositories of new knowledge as well as human capital. They are therefore potential sources of innovation and economic growth in both national and regional economies. However, their roles have changed significantly over the past three decades.

The impacts of universities on regional economic growth have been directly associated with their mere presence in the regions where they are located. These impacts are inextricably linked to universities' roles as regional employers, the regional demand they created for housing facilities and daily goods and services, and also their effects on capital investment. The roots of change lie in the economic slowdown suffered by the United States and Europe in the 1990s when universities were urged to contribute to regional economic competitiveness. After this time, universities began to enter into regional policy.

Since then, there has been a growing interest from academic researchers and policymakers on the role of universities in the regional development process. In an increasingly competitive and knowledge-based world economy, universities have been broadly perceived as crucial assets and pivotal actors in regional development policies. These policies have been mostly inspired by examples of dynamic university-led economic success, such as Route 128 and Silicon Valley in the United States for the Massachusetts Institute of Technology (MIT) and Stanford, respectively, and the "Golden Triangle" in the UK between Oxford, Cambridge and London.

But, more broadly, universities as facilitators of regional development policies were seen as offering potential to regions. Irrespective of different contexts and realities, there was a genuine belief, shared by academics as well as policymakers, in the ability of universities to transform regional economies.

This belief has developed into several conceptual models in recent years to better understand the contribution of universities to regional development.

These models are broadly based on a "one size fits all" approach and centred on a few successful regional experiences from developed economies through which a small, limited number of globally renowned universities served as case exemplars. Yet, this highlights the limitations of these models, not only regarding the complexity of the processes by which universities contribute to regional development, but also their application to peripheral regions. Although highly influential, these models have failed to capture and portray the diversity of regional contexts.

The relationship between university and region is bidirectional: the university shapes and, at the same time, is shaped by the region in which it operates. As universities are a mirror of their own societies, the social, economic, political and cultural context really matters. The impact of distinct regional settings, political environments for both higher education (HE) and territorial development, and also the types of universities (which are inherently complex and heterogeneous organizations) need to be taken into account by any model. Only then can we fully understand the dynamics of universities' regional engagement and their contribution to the development of regions.

Since the Covid-19 pandemic, universities have been at the forefront in responding to the crisis. This includes their work in medical and other essential research, producing personal protective equipment

https://doi.org/10.1080/2578711X.2021.1891764

(PPE), supplying student volunteers, and releasing medical and nursing students early to help deal with pressures in hospitals and medical facilities.

However, the crisis has also placed huge pressures on higher education institutions (HEIs) as well: through the necessity to switch to online teaching, challenges with student recruitment, especially international students, difficulties in conducting research, and creating a cohesive campus. This demonstrates only too well the closeness and interrelationships that universities can have in their home regions.

Equally, there is a real danger these become all-consuming and result in universities looking inwards, concerned about resources and breadth of activity, and scale back on wider engagement roles. As places grapple with the longer term socioeconomic impacts of Covid-19, universities will be critical actors. Understanding the dynamics and nuances of HE–region relationships is therefore needed now more than ever.

This Policy Expo book develops both a new universities and regional economic development policy framework, which we call *the ORPHIC Framework*, and a set of recommendations for universities and policymakers in order to understand the role and contribution of universities in regional development.

The book is structured as follows. Chapter 2 sets the scene by outlining the main ways in which universities can contribute to resilience and adaptation in regional economies. Chapter 3 analyses three university models that have shaped the discourse on universities in regional policy and practice. Chapter 4 then focuses on the commitment of universities to the regions in which they are located, exploring both the ways in which cooperative ties between universities and regional actors can be stimulated, and the drivers and challenges for regional engagement of universities. Chapter 5 outlines a new model, the ORPHIC Framework, that is aimed at policymakers to understand and assess the potential relationship between universities and regional development. Chapter 6 summarizes the key issues and concludes.

NOTE

[1] The terms "university" and "higher education" institution are used interchangeably throughout this book.

2. UNDERSTANDING THE CONTRIBUTIONS OF UNIVERSITIES TO REGIONAL DEVELOPMENT

Keywords: higher education, skills, knowledge, mission

2.1 INTRODUCTION

Universities, since the Middle Ages, have been set up with the purpose of meeting the demands of their societies. These demands varied according to the socioeconomic and political context of the time. This means that universities have had an extraordinary capacity for adaptation and reinvention throughout history. The world has changed and so have they.

But what are universities for? This simple question, which is as old as universities themselves, remains extremely topical and pertinent today. In fact, the rapid transformation experienced by contemporary societies implies the search for a better understanding of the role and purpose of universities. Due to the profound changes in the world economy, universities have been called upon to go beyond their traditional missions and therefore play a strategic role in the development process of their regions.

In order to act as strategic institutions and generate greater social and economic impacts on regional economies, universities must play multifaceted roles in the regions in which they operate. This chapter outlines the main ways in which universities can contribute to resilience and adaptation in regional economies.

2.2 EVOLUTION OF THE "IDEA" OF THE UNIVERSITY

The question "What are universities for?" has become an almost metaphysical one over the past century. Cardinal Newman's "idea" of the university was of a community of thinkers, learning for learning's sake rather than for any instrumental purpose, covering a broad range of liberal arts rather than narrow, scientific specialisms. While this philosophy might have resonated with faculty and students housed in the dreaming spires of the universities established in the medieval era, it was directly challenged by the founding of the so-called English civic universities[1] and US land-grant colleges[2] throughout the 19th century.

The primary function of these universities was to provide the research and skills for the new industries then emerging as a result of the agricultural and industrial revolutions, as well as the teachers and medical professionals needed to ensure an educated and healthy workforce,[3] and, as such, it heralded a move away from a Newmanist model of higher education.

While there has historically never been a singular accepted European model of higher education, the Humboldtian principle that emphasizes the "union of teaching and research" in academic work was dominant in German-speaking Europe, and highly influential in parts of Eastern Europe, from the late 1800s to the 1950s.[4] This principle contends that the function of the university was to advance knowledge by original and critical investigation, not just to transmit the legacy of the past or to teach skills.[5]

This philosophy of higher education arguably led to an emphasis on collaborative and applied research for the benefit of industry, the military and wider society in places that adopted the Humboldtian model. This was in contrast to the Newman model, which advocated a distinction between discovery and teaching, or the Napoleonic model which dominated in Southern Europe, where higher education was regulated and controlled by the state.

https://doi.org/10.1080/2578711X.2021.1891765

Since the mid-20th century, the centralization of higher education policy and increased public funding for research saw European universities move away from a focus on meeting the skills needs of their local economies,[6] while in the United States decentralized higher education and the dependence of public and private universities on local sources of funding meant that collaborative research relationships with industry became increasingly common.[7] The focus of universities' links with the "outside world" over the past 50 years has tended to be centred around the exploitation of research with the approach being an assisted linear model based on technology "push".[8]

This approach resulted in a considerable emphasis on the so-called "Triple Helix"[9] (see the Glossary), which emphasizes how the links between university, industry and government can drive innovation. In this framework, the stress has been on the role of research, particularly in scientific and technological fields. The emergence of the high-tech industries centred around Silicon Valley on the West Coast of the United States was seen as the embodiment of the success of this approach and one that policymakers around the world have sought to replicate (often with little success). This has led to a concentration of effort and resources on supporting collaborations between businesses and universities which generated "hard" outputs such as patent applications and business spin-offs, often to the neglect of developing the potential for "softer" impacts such as human capital and social.[10]

Although the landscape of higher education in Europe remains heterogeneous, the 20 years following the Bologna Process[11] have seen significant changes in cooperation between universities and business,[12] and there is a growing acceptance across European Union member states of the "new relevance" of universities to social and economic development.[13] This is underpinned by the Europe 2020 Growth Strategy and especially the emergence of the policy of Smart Specialisation[14] which gave increasing prominence to the role of universities not only in terms of the supply side (i.e., of research and skills) but also in supporting the demand side through capacity-building and supporting the governance of regional innovation.[15]

By the end of the first decade of the 21st century, this emphasis in public policy on the role of universities in explicitly contributing to social and economic development had continued to grow due to a number of concurrent factors. Some of these were driven by external global forces and trends; some were specific to local, regional and national policy contexts; and some were driven by changes in how universities are internally managed and led. This trend, if anything, accelerated in the 2010s and shows no evidence of slowing as we enter the third decade of the century.

This remains a policy conundrum at the European level and even beyond, led by organizations such as the Organisation for Economic Co-operation and Development (OECD) with its reviews of university–regional collaboration around the world, and is arguably most keenly felt in the UK, and in England in particular. This has manifested itself in recent years with UK government initiatives such as Science and Innovation Audits (aimed at mapping regional, largely university-led, research and innovation strengths) and the 2019 Civic University Commission. At the same time, the launch of a range of new funding schemes (e.g., the Industrial Strategy Challenge and Strength in Places funds) imply a leading role for (research-intensive) universities in addressing persistent and pervasive regional inequalities; most recently manifesting itself in policy terms as the "levelling up" agenda.

Today, universities (or higher education institutions—HEIs) are essential stakeholders in the context of the countries and regions in which they are located, promoting, in an articulated way, the improvement in levels of development and quality of life.

However, this commitment of universities to the places in which they are situated is relatively recent. While many universities as institutions date from the Middle Ages, their participation in actions and policies for local and regional development only began to occur in the last decades of the 20th century. For centuries, universities were seen as rather elitist institutions, closed in on themselves, with many performing their teaching and research functions without any meaningful connection to their own geographies.

The OECD has synthesized this behaviour very well:

In the past, neither public policy nor the higher education institutions themselves have tended to focus strategically on the contribution that they can make to the development of the regions where they are located. Particularly for older, traditional HEIs, the emphasis has often been on serving national goals or on the pursuit of knowledge with little regard for the surrounding environment.[16]

However, universities have been changing to meet the growing demands of society. This ability over time to change is, to a large extent, responsible for making universities recognized worldwide as repositories of knowledge, potential sources of innovation and drivers for nations' economic growth.

HEI missions, together with their local and regional impacts, depend on several factors, internal and external. Regardless of the impact level, it is noticeable that in the last few decades, the relationship between HEIs and their regions has been brought together more prominently with the objective of maximizing the impacts of their potential role within regions.[17]

HEIs differ from each other and regions differ as well. The focus, or the missions, of each university will also be different and, over time, become increasingly multifaceted, possibly incorporating new roles (Figure 2.1). This classification of university missions does not mean that all universities today only focus on University 4.0 or 5.0; rather, universities develop missions incrementally over time and are often at different stages of development.

As the economy and society evolve, new industrial and technological changes occur, through, for instance, the development of Internet of Things platforms, mobile devices, big data, augmented reality, cloud computing, and cybersecurity. Universities can play a pivotal role in this new economy through their role in advancing technology associated with, and even give rise to, spin-outs to high-tech industries. However, these technological developments, and how they impact upon places, are not uniform or linear in their effect.

Existing socioeconomic inequalities and regional asymmetries can interfere and shape how HEIs, researchers and students interact with University 4.0. The reasons for that can be varied: a lack of hardware, a lack of training, a lack of quality software, a lack of infrastructure and a lack of technical support. These have

  https://doi.org/10.1080/2578711X.2021.1891765

Figure 2.1 Development of university missions' focus over time.[18]

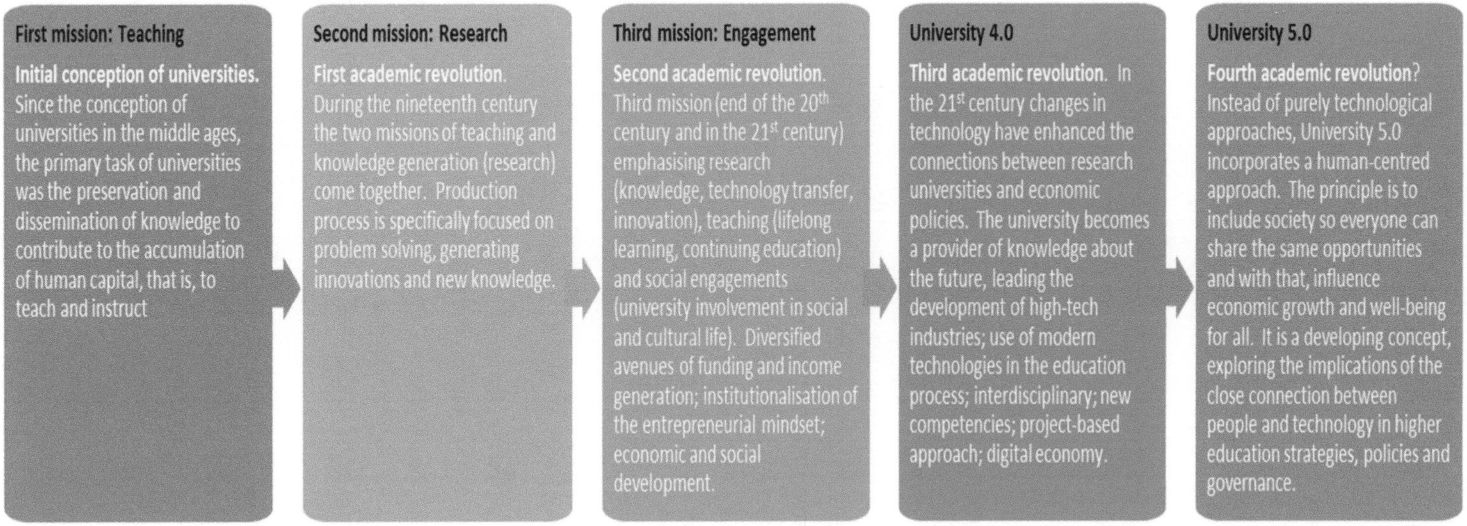

First mission: Teaching

Initial conception of universities. Since the conception of universities in the middle ages, the primary task of universities was the preservation and dissemination of knowledge to contribute to the accumulation of human capital, that is, to teach and instruct

Second mission: Research

First academic revolution. During the nineteenth century the two missions of teaching and knowledge generation ((research) come together. Production process is specifically focused on problem solving, generating innovations and new knowledge.

Third mission: Engagement

Second academic revolution. Third mission (end of the 20th century and in the 21st century) emphasising research (knowledge, technology transfer, innovation), teaching (lifelong learning, continuing education) and social engagements (university involvement in social and cultural life). Diversified avenues of funding and income generation; institutionalisation of the entrepreneurial mindset; economic and social development.

University 4.0

Third academic revolution. In the 21st century changes in technology have enhanced the connections between research universities and economic policies. The university becomes a provider of knowledge about the future, leading the development of high-tech industries; use of modern technologies in the education process; interdisciplinary; new competencies; project-based approach; digital economy.

University 5.0

Fourth academic revolution? Instead of purely technological approaches, University 5.0 incorporates a human-centred approach. The principle is to include society so everyone can share the same opportunities and with that, influence economic growth and well-being for all. It is a developing concept, exploring the implications of the close connection between people and technology in higher education strategies, policies and governance.

all been identified as barriers to the effective use of this technology in many places around the world. This is especially the case in peripheral and less developed countries.[19]

In developing regions, or in the most peripheral regions in economically advanced nations, the first mission, for example, will be essential for the qualification of the local and regional workforce, and may be the largest and most relevant mission expected by the region. This does not mean that universities do not strive for the second, third or fourth missions, but rather they may be secondary to current regional needs.

The more dynamic the regional productive structure, the greater the interaction with the HEIs it tends to be, and the more likely it will be that additional missions will be developed over time.

Many characteristics of HEIs influence the way they may develop the five missions. The way the HEI will transfer its cutting-edge research knowledge to the locality, or the possibility to be entrepreneurial, depends on an increase in the number of business incubation centres at the university or in partnership with other agencies.

This is highly dependent on a university's research and development (R&D) budget, but also on the number and diversity of its students in higher education, the demands of the specialized labour force in the region, and the existence of partnerships between universities and public–private institutions and industries.[20] It also depends on the alignment (or differences) between stakeholders and the goals of public and private universities, and what internal factors are affecting a university's business model, such as its structure, recruitment, strategic orientation, leadership and cultural values.

2.3 UNIVERSITIES AS REGIONAL ACTORS

Over the last 20 years, universities have become significant regional actors, taking on an important role in helping to develop the regions in which they are located. Within a knowledge-based economy, universities are no longer considered just creators and producers of knowledge, trainers of a skilled workforce that will become future citizens, or cultural disseminators. They are recognized as useful assets and strategic players in the successful economic growth and development of their home regions.

What led largely insular and secular universities to transform and change, becoming active and relevant players in promoting regional development? The reasons for this transition relate to the fact that universities, as with other regional organizations, are interested in promoting articulation between economic or social agents or citizens to achieve *a mutual interest in cooperation and collective trust.*

In recent decades, in most developed countries, public sector finances have suffered cuts in their funding. This has been the consequence of more restrictive levels of budgets, as well as the fact that the amount of public services has increased and diversified considerably. Those financial constraints have translated into difficulties for the public budgeting of universities in many countries at a time when the higher education sector has been growing.

This changed reality started to take place in the last decades of the 20th century—at the time with the expansion of higher education across the globe (Box 2.1)—and was accentuated at the beginning of the 21st century with the financial crisis and subsequent Great Recession of 2007–08. Following the Covid-19 pandemic in 2020 and beyond, we are once again witnessing upheaval across higher education as the disruption affects student migration (Box 2.2), international recruitment and examination entry processes with knock-on implications for university finances. Indirect impacts on higher education are also the consequence of:

Box 2.1 Where are higher education students in the world?

Figure 2.2 shows the increase in the number of enrolments in global higher education. It shows two major characteristics: the differences in the growth in the number of students in higher education in distinct groups of countries; and the structural change resulting from this, concerning the proportion of qualified human capital across various regions of the world.

Higher income countries comprised the majority until the mid-1980s, when they were surpassed in number by middle-income countries. At the beginning of the 21st century, they were again surpassed by upper middle- and lower middle-income countries.

Figure 2.2 shows that access to higher education is spreading to all regions, regardless of the income group. Growth has been much lower in low-income countries, and high-income countries have shown a slight decrease since 2011. These changes reflect changes in demographic evolution of the last few decades, with the more developed countries (with higher income levels) ageing. This is unlike those countries with intermediate levels of income and development, where the importance of young people has increased.

Figure 2.2 Enrolment in tertiary education by World Bank income groups, 1970–2018.[21]

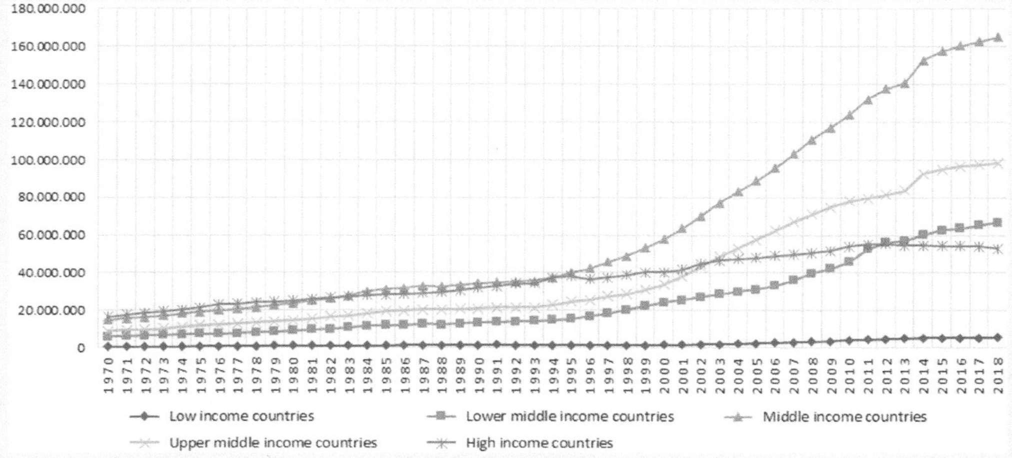

Box 2.2   The flow of internationally mobile students

Worldwide, countries have enhanced young people's school qualification attainment levels and, therefore, more by default, have reached the thresholds to enter higher education. As a result, most countries met the increased demand by their universities adopting robust responses. These developments have allowed a greater democratization in access to higher education and, in parallel with the growth of globalization and greater ease of travel between countries, higher education systems to become available to a wider cohort of international students.

Although Covid-19 may have affected international student mobility, universities have responded rapidly with a move to online learning and teaching platforms, thereby opening the possibility of remote teaching formats alongside any face-to-face contact.

In a context in which several developed countries have higher education systems with a higher capacity than the needs of the home student market, some universities have faced the challenge of enhanced global competition for students. The ability to attract and retain students to universities (whether home or overseas in origin) has been seen as one of the best ways to strengthen the university's link to regional economic development.

The internationalization process of higher education is increasingly more significant in relation to the challenges of globalization and regionalization in which the sector takes place. Although the internationalization agenda is not just about student mobility, it has been one of the most visible and impactful forms on many universities globally. Although higher education's internationalization aims to eliminate the barriers and frontiers of knowledge between nations, the process is not spatially balanced or homogeneous (Figure 2.3).

Figure 2.3   Net flow of internationally mobile students (inbound–outbound), 2017.[22]

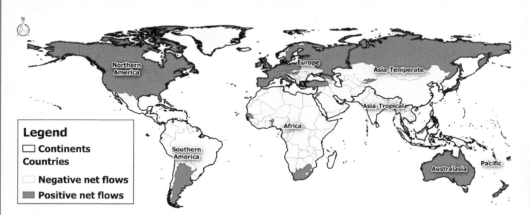

The northern hemisphere has two concentrations of countries: it is in these regions that universities in the developed countries have received the most international students with: the United States (898,332); UK (400,482); the Russian Federation (193,999; and France (169,001). The countries that send the most students to study abroad (and create a negative net flow in the process) are: Vietnam (-90,500); India (-285,330); and China (-770,982).

Australia is an exception in this analysis, as it is in the southern hemisphere, and was the third country with the highest positive balance in 2017 (367,707).

Many universities in the northern hemisphere can continue to function because of the large number of international students that the countries receive. On the other hand, the knowledge exchange within those countries that export students does improve, along with improvements in the educational abilities of their students. This has allowed national governments to fund overseas degrees and, in most cases such as China, contribute to the national economy on their return.

- the demands of wider nation-states' public policy, especially in the social domains of health, social care and employment support, which continue to demand significant proportion of state budgets; and

- gradual reduction in international student recruitment and mobility as registrations decrease year upon year.

The ongoing contraction in public funding to support HEI activities has led universities to seek other business models and external partners, both of which may contribute to enhancing and diversifying sources of financing. But these alternative business models have also led to universities paying more attention to greater liaisons with local and regional stakeholders, what is often referred to as the university's "third mission".

The third mission's effectiveness implies that the partners involved have mutuality: HEIs need to increase and diversify their sources of financing, while other regional partners need to have easier access to knowledge, innovation and technology. In this positive-sum game, which generates numerous territorial externalities, HEIs can participate through, for example, knowledge creation, improving human capital, supporting new business, providing policy and advice, paying taxes, or contributing to the cultural environment. In return, HEIs can receive—from regional and local stakeholders—student enrolment (retained or new numbers), finance for specialized research or consultancy, or requests for training and continual professional development.

To reinforce and support this mutuality, it is necessary to create an environment of trust between HEIs and other regional partners. Building institutional trust across sectors and agencies can be a time-consuming process. It does not happen simply through the signing of memoranda of understanding, but needs to be brokered and nurtured. For example, in low-density regions, where the number and diversity of stakeholders are small, the knowledge and confidence required for establishing institutional contacts is often easier to achieve, and based on existing webs of relations or personal interactions between the leaders of organizations.

2.4 HOW UNIVERSITIES CONTRIBUTE TO (REGIONAL) ECONOMIC DEVELOPMENT

From the mid-20th century, there has been an international trend for raising levels of participation in higher education.[23] This now means that universities, or other types of HEI, are a common feature of regions across the world. In the context of contemporary knowledge-based economies, these institutions are increasingly viewed as potential assets for place-based regional policies.[24] This is especially the case for universities located in regions where one of the key development challenges is increasing their share of innovative and high-skill industries.

Policymakers often act on the conviction that the research and teaching capabilities possessed within universities can be used to engender this growth in what are termed "peripheral" or "old industrial regions". In the academic literature, there is, however, an increasing recognition that the processes through which universities may contribute to local development are complex, and dependent on favourable conditions that will not be present in many regional contexts. The rest of this chapter begins to explore these processes and associated challenges by outlining the main ways in which HEIs can support the economy of their home region.

This section introduces three main areas of university activity and impact that underpin their contribution to resilience and adaptation in regional economies. The rest of the chapter then discusses each of these in more detail.

2.4.1 Anchoring local employment and expenditure

Its global expansion over recent decades now means that higher education is, in its own right, a sizable industry in many countries. For regions with a significant HEI presence, this brings a number of identifiable impacts for their local economies.[25] Universities are often now major employers of people across varied academic and non-academic occupations.

Furthermore, they also purchase a range of goods and services from suppliers who will include local businesses. At the larger end of the scale this can, for instance, include major investments in the construction of new buildings. Universities may also attract large numbers of domestic and international students to live in a city.

Students generate further economic impacts through their distinctive consumption patterns, demand for short-term rented housing and entry into local labour markets as part-time workers.[26] The economic multiplier effect means that the full extent of these sort of impacts will include further "induced" activity stimulated by first-order employment and expenditure. For instance, according to one analysis covering the whole of the UK in 2014–15, the estimated number of additional jobs supported through the spending of universities, their employees and international students (540,000) was notably higher than the number of people directly employed in the sector (404,000).[27]

2.4.2 Supplying graduates for regional labour markets

As institutions of tertiary education, the primary function that universities, colleges or technical institutes have in supporting the economy is the teaching of students who enter the labour market following their graduation. Higher education equips students with advanced knowledge in different specialized fields and enables them to develop a range of transferrable skills (e.g., technical, analytical, creative, communication, entrepreneurial, etc.) that are of value across a range of jobs in contemporary economies. These personal capabilities, in an aggregate form that economists call "human capital", are recognized as a driver of growth at the regional as well as national levels.[28] This has benefitted the economies of prospering cities that tend to have an above-average concentration of workers with a tertiary-level education.[29] They are also often net importers of graduates from other, less economically successful, places.

2.4.3 Enabling innovation through research and knowledge transfer

In many countries, universities are central actors within public research systems. The basic and applied research they perform across different scientific fields is a stimulus to the development of new technologies and other innovations taken up in industry and the public sector.[30] This transfer of knowledge occurs through varied means of engagement or collaboration with companies and/or commercialization of research by universities themselves or academic spin-out firms.[31] Publicly funded research also helps expand the capabilities for future innovation in the economic system. This occurs through the development of new scientific techniques and instruments, the training of highly skilled researchers, and the formation of networks between academics and industry.[32] The clearest manifestation of these "knowledge spillovers", as a regional development impact, is the emergence of clusters around universities in new high-tech or science-based industries.[33]

2.5 ANCHORING LOCAL EMPLOYMENT AND EXPENDITURE

The foundational role of universities in generating and sustaining wider activity within their local economies means they are sometimes referred to as *anchor institutions*.[34] As well as their size, this designation is based on the low likelihood that universities will relocate to another region (although some may open domestic or international branch campuses). Universities have also, traditionally, have had a level of financial security from a combination of, for example, public funding, student fees, estate holdings and endowments. This means, especially in comparison with organizations in the private sector, they are less vulnerable to suffering institutional failures that lead to closure, forced mergers or severe downsizing. This anchor institution characteristic may, however, be under threat for some universities due to a combination of moves towards market-based systems of higher education funding,[35] and by the unfolding effects of the Covid-19 pandemic on the sector.[36]

Nevertheless, the employment and expenditure impacts of large, locally embedded and financially secure universities can represent a source of stability in a regional economy. As the size of higher education sectors have expanded, they have become increasingly important within cities that have concurrently undergone decline of other industries.

For example, according to figures given in a recent report by the UPP Foundation, between 1978 and 2019, the number of people working in the steel industry in the northern British city of Sheffield fell from 45,000 to 3000. Over the same period, however, the number of students in Sheffield rose from 4000 to 60,000.[37] The two universities in the city are now—with public sector organizations such as the city council and National Health Service (NHS)—amongst the largest local employers with a combined number of 11,980 direct employees (10,420 full-time equivalent) in 2018–19.[38]

These mainly passive impacts can also be enhanced through procurement strategies that ensure a larger proportion of university expenditure remains in the local economy. For instance, this is an approach pioneered in the United States though the Evergreen Initiative in Cleveland, Ohio (Box 2.3).

Universities will often publicize employment and expenditure impacts as measurable evidence of the economic benefits they bring in return for public funding received. An overreliance on these multiplier effects will, however, be limited as an approach to the role of universities in regional policy. Beyond higher education itself, this contribution to the local economy will not be focused on the growth of knowledge-intensive industries that less-developed regions need to transform their economy towards higher productivity activities.

Much of the extra employment induced by the spending of universities, their staff and students will be in socially valuable, but relatively low-paid and insecure service jobs that are characteristic of post-industrial cities. The concentration of large numbers of students in certain neighbourhoods can also have negative social, cultural or housing displacement effects on local communities that counteract any economic benefits this group brings to a city.[39] Moreover, the employment and expenditure impacts of universities

---

Box 2.3   Harnessing the procurement power of local anchor institutions: The Evergreen Initiative

In 2008, a group of local institutions came together to facilitate an economic breakthrough in Cleveland, Ohio. They aimed to create a more sustainable, green economy in a post-industrial city that had experienced population decline and capital flight over several decades. The Evergreen Initiative set out to harness the spending power of city anchor institutions such as universities and hospitals, which are specifically tied to a local economy and cannot "get up and leave". Cleveland adopted a model of community wealth-building as an alternative to the dominant "trickle down" model, which often relies on inward investments, where public subsidy is used to entice multinational corporations to set up in a city, often resulting in low-wage jobs, with business profit also leaving the local area.

To achieve the Evergreen Initiative's economic development aims, a group of cooperative businesses was formed designed to deliver specific services that would meet the growing demand from anchor institutions and create living-wage jobs in six low-income neighbourhoods through employment, investment and business development. These included a laundry, a renewable energy company, and a fruit-and-vegetable producer.

The Evergreen Initiative has re-engaged local people in the economy to support local employment, investment and increase the circulation of capital in Cleveland, addressing the multiple socioeconomic challenges from the area's large-scale industrial change. It has created successful local businesses that re-invest in the local community, creating new job opportunities, particularly for those who are furthest from the job market.

The project has social good at its heart, and through local, worker-owned job creation, and sustainable, green and democratic workplaces, it ultimately aims to ensure that the benefits of economic growth in Cleveland are equitable. Importantly, the project has successfully harnessed the spending power of its big local anchor institutions to stabile and revitalize disinvested communities through procurement programmes and cooperatives.[40]

---

are largely separate from their qualitatively more important functions for regional development that arise from research and education activities.

Recent academic and policy thinking has sought to understand strong regional economies as those that are *resilient* to "shocks" in the wider national or global economy. As higher education has proved to be less vulnerable to previous economic downturns or structural transformations than many other industries (including parts of the public sector), cities or towns with large anchor universities will benefit from an extra buffer of steady employment and expenditure. This, in turn, may help them to withstand or even recover from these shocks better than those typically smaller cities or towns that do not have a significant HEI presence.

However, the academic studies have come to emphasize that the most resilient regional economies are those that are best able to *adapt* to global competition and technological change on an ongoing basis.[41] It is in helping to expand this adaptive capacity for change over time that university education and research can make their more significant inputs to the long-term success of regional economies.

2.6 SUPPLYING GRADUATES FOR REGIONAL LABOUR MARKETS

The primary value of higher education for regional development is in increasing knowledge and skills in the local labour force. The accumulation of human capital is a dynamic that encourages continual transformation in a regional economy by raising levels of *labour productivity* (of highly educated individuals and their co-workers), *innovation* (through enabling the quicker generation and adoption of new technologies) and *entrepreneurship* (via individuals with the ideas, skills and access to resources to start new-growth companies).[42] These human capital effects therefore expand the adaptive capacity of the regional economy.[43] This is supported by empirical evidence that metropolitan regions in the United States, with larger numbers of university graduates in science, technology, engineering and mathematics (STEM) subjects, had stronger productivity growth during the period (2007–09) of the Great Recession.[44]

The importance of a local supply of graduates is such that the foundation of a university in a peripheral city can itself be a regional policy intervention with positive effects on human capital and productivity.[45] In some deindustrialized cities, such as Pittsburgh in the US Rust Belt, the presence of large universities may also be associated with growing numbers of young, educated workers who are helping to slow or reverse patterns of urban decline and population loss.[46]

The major challenge for these different types of less-developed regions, however, is increasing their retention of graduates from local universities. A key process shaping the economic geography of any country is the internal migration of highly skilled people.[47] This mobility is very high amongst those who have recently graduated from university, especially if they had previously moved from their home region to study.[48]

Studies from multiple countries have shown that, on balance, the resulting migration flows clearly favour core cities and regions where there are better career opportunities for graduates.[49] These patterns of so-called "brain drain" can therefore undermine the benefits that the educational function of universities bring to the economies of less-developed regions. This is particularly so when these institutions have a large intake of highly mobile students from outside their home region.

By working in partnership with local policymakers and businesses, universities can take steps to boost levels of graduate retention. This can be achieved through actions, for instance, to connect students to regional small and medium-sized enterprises (SMEs), encourage graduate entrepreneurship or involve universities in strategies to grow the local technology sector.[50] Another approach may advocate universities more closely matching their educational provision to the needs of local employers.[51]

The danger of this, however, is that it can reinforce an existing "low skills equilibrium" in less-developed regions rather than helping to generate the new, more knowledge-intensive jobs needed to upgrade the local labour market.[52] This is why wider regional policy measures to support the expansion of knowledge-intensive industries are required to work in conjunction with efforts to increase graduate retention. Indeed, there is evidence that the spillover effects that academic R&D activities have within a regional economy can help to attract human capital by raising demand for high-skilled labour in technical or scientific fields.[53]

2.7 ENABLING INNOVATION THROUGH RESEARCH AND KNOWLEDGE TRANSFER

The distinctive societal function of universities in carrying out more exploratory forms of basic research (often alongside other public research organizations) is crucial to the development of long-term adaptive capacity in national and regional economies.[54] In exceptional cases, the innovation generated through these activities can lead to a region developing new economic paths based on radically different technologies.[55]

For instance, the US city of Pittsburgh has been widely recognized for its transition from a dependence on a declining steel industry to a post-industrial economy, in which high-technology sectors such as advanced manufacturing and life and health sciences have been drivers of recovery.[56] This process has been brokered by enterprising local political and business leaders, but it has drawn heavily on the strong research universities, hospitals and other institutional assets that exist in the city.[57]

The contribution of universities to regional adaptation can, however, also be focused on enabling the transformation of traditional industries through processes of technological upgrading or diversification. These different forms of path development may entail different mechanisms of engagement. The indigenous creation of new industries implies a focus on the formation of enterprises through university spin-outs.

On the other hand, technological upgrading or diversification is more likely to require academics to interact with existing firms through knowledge-transfer channels such as research collaborations, consultancy or staff/student secondments.[58] The second of these approaches is the focus of the Advanced Manufacturing Research Centre (AMRC) of the University of Sheffield in the UK (Box 2.4).

The need for universities to fulfil these roles in regional innovation policies is especially pronounced in less-developed regions where R&D capabilities in the private sector and other parts of the public sector may be lacking. Even where areas of academic research excellence do exist in universities outside of core

   https://doi.org/10.1080/2578711X.2021.1891765

Box 2.4   University of Sheffield's Advanced Manufacturing Research Centre (AMRC)

The AMRC was established by the University of Sheffield and Boeing in 2001 as a centre of excellence in academic–industry collaboration. It is located on an advanced manufacturing park outside of Sheffield, UK, and now employs over 500 researchers and engineers. Since 2011, it has been part of a UK network of national technology and innovation "Catapult" centres in high-value manufacturing. The AMRC interacts with manufacturing companies of different sizes to give them access to advanced expertise and R&D capabilities in such areas as high-performance machining, composite materials and digitalization. For SMEs, this is done through channels including short demonstrator projects with individual companies, collaborative research projects involving a consortium of partners, and programmes focused on helping members become part of specialist supply chains. The AMRC works with manufacturers throughout the UK (and now has branches in Preston and north Wales), but it does bring specific extra benefits for its home region. For instance, it runs an engineering apprenticeship training course focused predominantly on young people and employers in the Sheffield City Region. The AMRC has also attracted companies to locate on the advanced manufacturing park, including the recent opening of manufacturing facilities by two of its long-term partners, Boeing and McLaren.[59]

Box 2.5   Barriers to regional development impacts from academic research[60]

- Critical mass: the scale of excellent research in universities is not large enough, or too fragmented between different fields, to generate significant knowledge spillovers.
- Motivation: a lack of incentives for universities and/or academics to work with industry and other stakeholders in their region.
- Misalignment: little connection between the scientific focus of research activities in universities and industrial specializations in the region.
- Absorptive capacity: the narrow scope for local firms (especially SMEs) to engage with and make use of the advanced knowledge generated by research in universities due to the comparatively underdeveloped nature of their existing technology and human capital.
- Intermediaries: gaps in the translational capability needed to effectively coordinate university–industry collaborations and facilitate knowledge transfer.

regions, however, there is no guarantee that this will translate into innovation within their local economy.[61] This is due to a set of common barriers that are identified in Box 2.5.

These barriers highlight the need to develop regional innovation systems in which the *supply-side*, *demand-side* and *translational* dimensions of knowledge transfer between universities and businesses are all present.[62] Addressing factors limiting the demand to interact with universities on the part of local firms, such as *misalignment* and *absorptive capacity*, are key challenges in many less-developed regions. In these cases, research universities are more likely to look outside of their home region to work with firms that have the requisite absorptive capacity to make their collaboration mutually beneficial.[63]

By contrast, the concentration of high-technology industries in certain geographical centres (e.g., cities such as Boston, San Francisco and Seattle in the United States) leads to a virtuous circle of increasing demand for connections into local universities from a growing population of innovative firms.[64] However, the main productive industries in less-developed regions are often those that innovate incrementally through applied problem-solving and learning-by-doing with suppliers and customers, rather than through an R&D-driven process that depends on collaboration with universities.[65]

In such contexts, the role of universities within "smart" regional innovation policies should be oriented towards a means of engagement that will help these existing industries transform themselves by upgrading their technology or diversifying into new markets.[66]

2.8 CONCLUSIONS

This chapter has outlined the ways in which universities can help regional economies become more resilient and adaptive to change through their employment and expenditure, education programmes and research activities. At the same time, however, it has also highlighted several challenges commonly encountered with these processes in less-developed regions.

For these barriers to be overcome, it is necessary for universities to be *actively* engaged in the development of these regions. This is instead of expecting meaningful results to come about as a side effect of their core teaching and research functions, or from the socioeconomic impacts generated by their presence as anchor institutions. For instance, this could be achieved by universities taking steps to target procurement towards local suppliers, increase graduate retention in their home city or undertaking collaborative R&D that is oriented towards the industrial base of the region.

The next chapter will explore the different forms that this shift in institutional orientation can take in more depth and in the context of regional policy internationally.

NOTES

[1] Goddard J (2009) *Reinventing the Civic University*. London: National Endowment for Science, Technology and the Arts (NESTA).

[2] McDowell G (2003) Engaged universities: Lessons from the land-grant universities and extension. *Annals of the American Academy of Political and Social Science*, 585(1): 31–50.

[3] Delanty G (2002) The university and modernity: A history of the present. In K Robins and F Webster (eds.), *The Virtual University? Information, Markets and Managements*, pp. 31-48. Oxford: Oxford University Press.

[4] Healy A, Perkmann M, Goddard J and Kempton L (2014) *Measuring the Impact of University–Business Cooperation: Final Report*. Brussels: Directorate General for Education and Culture, European Commission.

[5] Anderson R (2004) *European Universities from the Enlightenment to 1914*. Oxford: Oxford University Press.

[6] Goddard (2009), see Reference 1.

[7] Mowrey D (1999) *The Evolving Structure of University–Industry Collaboration in the United States: Three Cases*. Washington, DC: National Academies Press.

[8] European Commission (2011) *Connecting Universities to Regional Growth: A Practical Guide*. Brussels: European Commission.

[9] Etzkowitz H (2008) *The Triple Helix: University–Industry–Government Innovation in Action*. London: Routledge.

[10] Science Business Innovation Board (2012) *Making Industry–University Partnerships Work—Lessons from Successful Collaborations*. Brussels: Science Business Innovation Board AISBL.

[11] The Bologna Process was launched in 1999 by the education ministers of 29 European countries in an attempt to bring coherence to higher education systems across the continent.

[12] Technopolis (2011) *University–Business Cooperation: 15 Institutional Case Studies on the Links between Higher Education Institutions and Businesses*. Brussels: Technopolis Group.

[13] European Universities Association (2006) *The Rise of Knowledge Regions: Emerging Opportunities and Challenges for Universities*. Brussels: European University Association.

[14] Smart Specialisation is the new iteration of European regional innovation strategies, the development of which became an *ex-ante* conditionality for regions to access European Structural and Investment Funds in the 2014–20 programming period.

[15] Goddard J, Kempton L and Vallance P (2013) Universities and Smart Specialisation: Challenges, tensions and opportunities for the innovation strategies of European regions. *Ekonomiaz. Revista vasca de Economia*, 83(2): 83-102.

[16] Organisation for Economic Co-operation and Development (OECD) (2007) *Higher Education and Regions: Globally Competitive, Locally Engaged*. Paris: OECD.

[17] Drucker J and Goldstein H (2007) Assessing the regional economic development impacts of universities: A review of current approaches. *International Regional Science Review*, 30: 20–46. doi:10.1177/0160017606296731; Addie J-PD (2017) From the urban university to universities in urban society. *Regional Studies*, 51(7): 1089–1099. doi:10.1080/00343404.2016.1224334.

[18] Sources: Adapted from Mora J-G, Serra MA and Vieira M-J (2018) Social engagement in Latin American Universities. *Higher Education Policy*, 31: 513-534; Shah SI, Shahjehan A and Afsar B (2019) Determinants of entrepreneurial university culture under unfavorable conditions: Findings from a developing country. *Higher Education Policy*, 32: 249–271; Kretz A and Sá C (2013) Third stream, fourth mission: Perspectives on university engagement with economic relevance. *Higher Education Policy*, 26: 497-506; Madaliyeva Z, Kassen G, Sadykova N, Baimoldina L and Zakaryanova S (2020) Resources and competencies as major determinants of university models 4.0. Paper presented at the E3S Web of Conferences, 159, 09001. doi:10.1051/e3sconf/202015909001.

[19] Ali AH and Mohammad OKJ (2019) Impacting of the e-platforms on the 4.0th industrial educational revolution. In *Proceedings of the 9th International Conference on Information Systems and Technologies (ICIST 2019)*, art. 29. New York: Association for Computing Machinery. https://doi.org/10.1145/3361570.3361608; Madaliyeva Z, Kassen G, Sadykova N, Baimoldina L, and Zakaryanova S (2020) Resources and competencies as major determinants of university models 4.0. Paper presented at the E3S Web of Conferences, 159: 09001. doi:10.1051/e3sconf/202015909001.

[20] Shah et al. (2019), see Reference 18.

[21] Source: Adapted from UNESCO (2020). Available at: http://data.uis.unesco.org/index.aspx?queryid=3820) [Accessed 28 May 2020].

[22] Source: Adapted from UNESCO (2020), see Reference 21.

[23] Schofer E and Meyer JW (2005) The worldwide expansion of higher education in the twentieth century. *American Sociological Review*, 70(6): 898–920.

[24] Beer A, McKenzie F, Blazek J, Sotarauta M and Ayers S (2020) What are the benefits of place-based policy? *Regional Studies Policy Impact Books*, 2(1): 23–38.

[25] Goddard J and Vallance P (2013) *The University and the City*. London: Routledge.

[26] Munro M, Turok I and Livingston M (2009) Students in cities: A preliminary analysis of their patterns and effects. *Environment and Planning A*, 41(8): 1805–1825.

[27] Oxford Economics (2017) *The Economic Impact of Universities in 2014–2015: Report for Universities UK*. Oxford: Oxford Economics.

[28] Faggian A, Modrego F and McCann P (2019) Human capital and regional development. In R Capello and P Nijkamp (eds.), *Handbook of Regional Growth and Development Theories*, pp. 149–171. Cheltenham: Edward Elgar.

[29] Glaeser EL and Saiz A (2004) The rise of the skilled city. *Brookings-Wharton Papers on Urban Affairs*, 2004(1): 47–105.

[30] Rosenberg N and Nelson RR (1994) American universities and technical advance in industry. *Research Policy*, 23(3): 323–348.

[31] Perkmann M, Tartari V, McKelvey M, Autio E, Brostrom A, D'Este P, Fini R, Geuna A, Grimaldi R, Hughes A, Krabel S, Kitson M, Llerena P, Lissoni F, Salter A and Sobrero M (2013) Academic engagement and commercialisation: a review of the literature on university–industry relations. *Research Policy*, 42(2): 423–442.

[32] Salter AJ and Martin BR (2001) The economic benefits of publicly funded basic research: A critical review. *Research Policy*, 30(3): 509–532.

[33] Garnsey E and Lawton SH (1998) Proximity and complexity in the emergence of high-technology industry: The Oxbridge comparison. *Geoforum*, 29(4): 433–450; Wolfe DA (2005) The role of universities in regional development and cluster formation. In GA Jones, PL McCarney and ML Skolnik (eds.), *Creating Knowledge, Strengthening Nations: The Changing Role of Higher Education*, pp. 167–194. Toronto: University of Toronto Press; Patton D and Kenney M (2010) The role of the university in the genesis and evolution of research-based clusters. In D Fornahl, S Henn and M-P Menzel (eds.), *Emerging Clusters: Theoretical, Empirical and Political Perspectives on the Initial Stage of Cluster Evolution*, pp. 214–238. Cheltenham: Edward Elgar.

[34] Harris M and Holley K (2016) Universities as anchor institutions: Economic and social potential for urban development. In MB Paulsen (ed.), *Higher Education: Handbook of Theory and Research: Volume 31*, pp. 393–439. Heidelberg: Springer.

[35] Goddard J, Coombes M, Kempton L and Vallance P (2014) Universities as anchor institutions in cities in a turbulent funding environment: Vulnerable institutions and vulnerable places in England. *Cambridge Journal of Regions, Economy and Society*, 7(2): 307–325.

[36] Halterbeck M, Conlon G, Williams R and Miller J (2020) *Impact of the Covid-19 Pandemic on University Finances: Report for the University and College Union*. London: London Economics.

[37] UPP Foundation (2019) *Truly Civic: Strengthening the Connection between Universities and Their Places*. London: UPP Foundation.

[38]Figures are from https://www.hesa.ac.uk/data-and-analysis/staff/working-in-he [Accessed 16 August 2020].

[39]Smith DP (2005) Studentification: The gentrification factory? In R Atkinson and G Bridge (eds.), *Gentrification in a Global Context: The New Urban Colonialism*, pp.73–90. London: Routledge.

[40]Source: Localize West Midlands. Available at: http://localisewestmidlands.org.uk/2019/community-economic-development-in-action-the-cleveland-model.

[41]Pike A, Dawley S and Tomaney J (2010) Resilience, adaptation, and adaptability. *Cambridge Journal of Regions, Economy and Society*, 3(1): 59–70; Boschma R (2015) Towards an evolutionary perspective on regional resilience. *Regional Studies*, 49(5): 733–751; Martin R and Sunley P (2015) On the notion of regional economic resilience: Conceptualization and explanation. *Journal of Economic Geography*, 15(1): 1–42.

[42]Mathur VK (1999) Human capital-based strategy for regional economic development. *Economic Development Quarterly*, 13(3): 203–216.

[43]Glaeser EL (2005) Reinventing Boston: 1630–2003. *Journal of Economic Geography*, 5(2): 119–153.

[44]Lendel I and Qian H (2017) Inside the great recession: University products and regional economic development. *Growth and Change*, 48(1): 153–173.

[45]Andersson R, Quigley JM and Wilhelmson M (2004) University decentralization as regional policy: The Swedish experiment. *Journal of Economic Geography*, 4(4): 371–388; Evers G (2019) The impact of the establishment of a university in a peripheral region on the local labour market for graduates. *Regional Studies, Regional Science*, 6(1): 319–330.

[46]Hartt M, Zwick A and Revington N (2019) Resilient shrinking cities. In MA Burayidi, A Allen, J Twigg and C Wamsler (eds.), *The Routledge Handbook of Urban Resilience*, pp.172–183. Abingdon: Routledge.

[47]Faggian et al. (2019), see Reference 28.

[48]Kodrzycki YK (2001) Migration of recent college graduates: Evidence from the national longitudinal survey of youth. *New England Economic Review*, January–February: 13–34.

[49]Hoare A and Corver M (2010) The regional geography of new young graduate labour in the UK. *Regional Studies*, 44(4): 477–494; Marinelli E (2013) Sub-national graduate mobility and knowledge flows: An exploratory analysis of onward- and return-migrants in Italy. *Regional Studies*, 47(10): 1618–1633; Benneworth P and Herbst M (2015) The city as a focus for human capital migration: Towards a dynamic analysis of university human capital contributions. *European Planning Studies*, 23(3): 452–474.

[50]Foresight (2016) *Future of Cities: Graduate Mobility and Productivity*. London: Government Office for Science.

[51]Chatterton P and Goddard J (2000) The response of higher education institutions to regional needs. *European Journal of Education*, 35(4): 475–496.

[52]Arbo P and Benneworth P (2007) *Understanding the Regional Contribution of Higher Education Institutions: A Literature Review*. Paris: Organisation for Economic Co-operation and Development (OECD).

[53]Abel JR and Deitz R (2012) Do colleges and universities increase their region's human capital? *Journal of Economic Geography*, 12(3): 667–691.

[54]Vallance P (2016) Universities, public research, and evolutionary economic geography. *Economic Geography*, 92(4): 355–377.

[55]Gilbert BA and Campbell JT (2015) The geographic origins of radical technological paradigms: A configurational study. *Research Policy*, 44(2): 311–327.

[56]Andes S, Horowitz M, Helwig R and Katz B (2017) *Capturing the Next Economy: Pittsburgh's Rise as a Global Innovation City*. Washington, DC: Brookings Institute.

[57]MacKinnon D et al. (2019) Rethinking path creation: A geographical political economy approach. *Economic Geography*, 95(2): 113–135.

[58]Lester RK (2005) *Universities, innovation, and the competitiveness of local economies: A summary report from the Local Innovation Systems Project—Phase 1* (Working Paper No. 05-010). Cambridge, MA: MIT Industrial Performance Center; Gjelsvik M (2018) Universities, innovation and competitiveness in regional economies. *International Journal of Technology Management*, 76(1–2): 10–31.

[59]Sources: AMRC website, https://www.amrc.co.uk/; Breach A (2019) *Parks and Innovation: Lessons from Sheffield's Advanced Manufacturing Park*. London: Centre for Cities.

[60]Source: Bonaccorsi A (2017) Addressing the disenchantment: Universities and regional development in peripheral regions. *Journal of Economic Policy Reform*, 20(4): 293–320.

[61]Power D and Malmberg A (2008) The contribution of universities to innovation and economic development: In what sense a regional problem? *Cambridge Journal of Regions, Economy and Society*, 1(2): 233–245.

[62]Marques P, Morgan K, Healy A and Vallance P (2019) Spaces of novelty: can universities play a catalytic role in less developed regions? *Science and Public Policy*, 46(5): 763–771.

[63]Muscio A (2013) University–industry linkages: What are the determinants of distance in collaborations? *Papers in Regional Science*, 92(4): 715–739.

[64]Atkinson RD, Muro M and Whiton J (2019) *The Case for Growth Centers: How to Spread Tech Innovation Across America*. Washington, DC: Brookings Institute.

[65]Isaksen A and Karlsen J (2010) Different modes of innovation and the challenge of connecting universities and industry: Case studies of two regional industries in Norway. *European Planning Studies*, 18(12): 1993–2008.

[66]Vallance P, Blažek J, Edwards J and Květoň V (2018) Smart Specialisation in regions with less-developed research and innovation systems: A changing role for universities? *Environment and Planning C: Politics and Space*, 36(2): 219–238.

3. EXAMINING UNIVERSITY MODELS IN REGIONAL DEVELOPMENT

Keywords: universities, entrepreneurship, engagement, system-based

3.1 INTRODUCTION

The impetus for universities to be more active participants in the development of their regions has raised questions about how this additional demand can be met through their institutional strategies, structures, and educational or research programmes.[1] In response, a number of conceptual models of universities as institutional actors in regional development have gained currency in the academic literature.

This chapter outlines the defining features (and limitations) of three of these models—*entrepreneurial*, *engaged* and *system based*—that are common to previous typologies of universities.[2] These three models are notable for shaping the discourse around universities in regional policy practice on an international level, which transcend the specific higher education contexts of individual countries. The chapter identifies some of the transnational organizations, networks and other mechanisms through which they have been widely spread and popularized as policy ideas.

3.2 THE ENTREPRENEURIAL UNIVERSITY

The concept of an *entrepreneurial university* has been developed in higher education studies to help understand the ways in which institutions adapt to changes in their environment. For instance, some commentators have viewed entrepreneurial universities as those that pursue a more diverse set of income streams, in response to declining levels of public funding for higher education relative to growing student numbers.[3]

Other interpretations have focused on managerial, organizational and cultural transformations that accompany the growing expectation that universities should fulfil a "third mission", one focused on their contribution to the knowledge-based economy.[4] This perspective has a clear resonance with the increasing role ascribed to universities in regional economic development. In particular, the entrepreneurial university model foregrounds steps taken by higher education institutions (HEIs) to commercialize their knowledge through such channels as the licensing of intellectual property, academic or student spin-out companies, and partnerships with industry.

These behaviours have been widely encouraged in the United States since the landmark Bayh–Dole Act of 1980 that made it easier for universities to patent the results of research funded by the federal government.[5] Equivalent policies (modified for varying higher education systems) have subsequently been adopted by governments in other advanced economies.[6]

One effect of this is that research universities throughout the world now have technology-transfer strategies and specialist administrative staff to help manage the commercialization process. Also commonplace are university-based start-up incubators and/or science and technology parks that support academic spin-outs and other knowledge-intensive enterprises. An entrepreneurial university can also be analysed as an environment that integrates values of innovation and knowledge creation into its educational practices, and actively encourages the entrepreneurship of students and graduates.[7]

https://doi.org/10.1080/2578711X.2021.1891767

As discussed in chapter 2, the commercialization of academic knowledge can be the catalyst for the emergence of clusters in science or technology-based industries.

Academic spin-out firms have been a key mechanism through which these clusters can start to grow around strong research universities.[8] High numbers of spin-outs can have a cumulative effect when they support the formation of specialist labour markets and second-generation spin-off firms.[9]

University (or graduate) spin-outs also often maintain strong links with their parent institution, and are therefore able to benefit from ongoing research collaborations and knowledge spillovers.[10] This can be especially important in building innovation ecosystems in less developed regions. Spin-out firms will typically have higher than average capacities to absorb new knowledge from universities and help transfer this to other companies.[11]

The dominant narratives of regional economic growth with entrepreneurial universities at their centre are, however, mainly predicated on the experience of select institutions in stronger regional economies. Most notably, these include US cases that were early pioneers in developing higher education links to industry. For example, companies with strong research or alumni ties to Stanford University (including tenants on its Stanford Research Park) were integral to the post-war emergence and subsequent growth of high-technology industry in Silicon Valley.[12] This institution (along with the University of California Berkeley in the San Francisco Bay area) continues to nurture the innovation ecosystem that has formed in this region through its support for academic and graduate enterprise and attraction of researchers and students from around the world.[13]

On the East Coast, Massachusetts Institute of Technology (MIT) also has a strong tradition of encouraging entrepreneurialism amongst its faculty and students. Recently, this approach to local development has been translated into a set of best practices and exported to cities and countries globally, through the MIT Regional Entrepreneurship Acceleration Programme (REAP).[14]

These two examples of research-intensive entrepreneurial universities informed the development of the so-called "triple helix" framework.[15] Here, universities are given equal standing to businesses and government as one of the three core types of actor in knowledge-based economies.

As well as gaining traction as an academic concept, the triple helix framework has entered the global lexicon of economic development policy as an expedient way of talking about the complex and collaborative nature of innovation processes based on systemic relationships between different forms of organization within a given territory.[16] Its appeal across a range of national and regional contexts can be seen in the growth of the Triple Helix Association which, since 1996, has held regular international conferences for scholars and practitioners in cities across Europe, North and South America, Asia, and Africa.[17]

This international popularization of the triple helix framework has seen the entrepreneurial university and related concepts used in application to a wider range of geographical settings and development challenges. In other contexts, it has been argued that universities can utilize an entrepreneurial approach to manage more effectively their relationships with a broader range of external stakeholders, including local civic and community actors.[18]

As a model underpinning regional development policy, however, the defining feature of entrepreneurial universities remains the priority they attach to the commercialization of academic research. A key criticism of this is that it presents a narrow view of the varied means through which HEIs can contribute to their regional economies (as discussed in chapter 2).

At the level of their individual employees, surveys of academics have demonstrated that other means of interaction with the outside world—for example, related to public/community engagement or collaborative research—are far more widely practiced in the academy than those related to commercialization.[19] Empirical evidence also indicates that only a small proportion of universities have technology-transfer programmes that are successful to the extent that they generate a meaningful financial return for the institution.[20]

A focus on the generation of new industries through academic commercialization may not, therefore, be a policy approach that is appropriately targeted at less developed regions. For these contexts, in particular, other models of the regional roles of universities are needed.

3.3 THE ENGAGED UNIVERSITY

In relation to entrepreneurial models, the concept of an *engaged university* can be defined by the involvement of HEIs in a broader range of activities with external actors.[21] This model encompasses commercialization and technology-transfer roles, but also contributions to local and regional development through workforce training, providing consultancy to businesses, advising governments in the formulation of public policy, and economic or social engagement with community groups.[22] This recognizes that the roles universities play in their regions do not have to be directly *generative* of new commercial activity based on knowledge capital, but can be *developmental* of wider capacities in areas such as human capital, interorganizational networks and local governance.[23]

This engaged university model also lends itself to a more holistic view of potential HEI contributions to local and regional development. Here, the extensive engagement by academics in fields such as medical and life sciences, renewable and/or low carbon energy, digital technologies and the arts, can contribute to addressing societal challenges locally as well as creating new market opportunities for businesses in the region.[24]

This local engagement can be taken further when universities use their home cities as "living laboratories" to trial experimental interventions in such areas as urban sustainability or public health.[25] As an institution and community of academics and students, a university is also firmly embedded within the cultural ecosystems of its region and one that supports both not-for-profit arts organizations and businesses in the creative industries.[26]

A key argument underlying the engaged university model is that the increasing recognition of the economic and social value that HEIs can bring to their regions is driving expectations that their teaching and research should be responsive to the needs of local industries, labour markets, and governmental or civil society actors.[27] This resonates with recent appeals for the "civic" mission—which was central to the foundation of US and UK universities in the 19th and early 20th centuries—to be revitalized as a guiding principle for contemporary higher education.[28] As well as this Anglo-American *civic university*, other normative expressions of a socially engaged university model have been proposed in different geographical settings. For example, the *responsible university* in the Nordic countries;[29] and the *developmental university* in the Global South.[30]

At the same time, the engaged university is a concept with enough universal resonance to be applicable internationally.[31] This has been put into practice with the growth of the Talloires Network of over 400 HEIs in 78 countries that work together to strengthen their civic roles and social responsibilities.[32] The Organisation for Economic Co-operation and Development (OECD) has also been active in promoting a holistic vision of "globally competitive" but "locally engaged" universities through a series of reviews of higher education in regional and city development.[33] Across three rounds between 2005 and 2012, these reviews were conducted in over 30 regions from across OECD member countries.[34]

Another key argument associated with this approach is that instead of being marginalized as a separate and discretionary "third mission", regional engagement needs to be embedded in the core research and teaching activities of universities. This is illustrated in the models of "un-civic" and "civic" universities (Figures 3.1 and 3.2).

Figure 3.1 The "un-civic" university.[35]

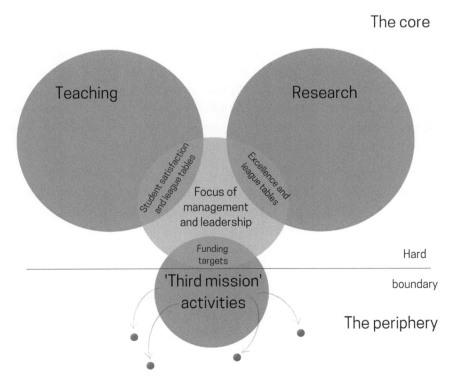

Figure 3.2 The "civic" university.[36]

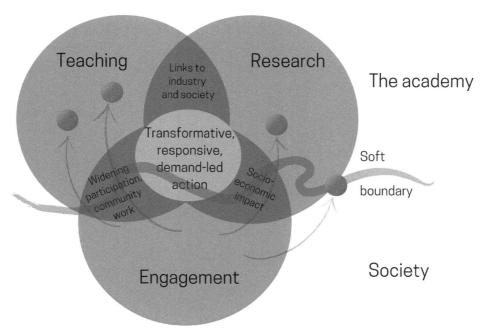

Goddard et al. (2016) depict the "un-civic university" as one in which the two core missions of teaching and research are most pivotal, though treated as unconnected activities by university leadership.[37] "Third mission" activities are seen as peripheral, particularly if there are no funding targets associated with them. This means that in the un-civic university there is a hard boundary separating what is seen as core and non-core activity, with support mechanisms directed only towards the former. In the "civic" university, all three missions are seen as equally important and mutually reinforcing. Rather than a hard boundary between the core and periphery, there is a soft and permeable boundary between the university and society in general, with activities across each domain valued and supported by the institution.

As with debates around the entrepreneurial university model, a crucial question that follows is how this engagement can be institutionalized within the management and organizational structures of universities.[38] Following from this, a major challenge facing engaged university models is explaining how regional development needs can be prioritized by institutions that operate in higher education and public research environments and that are primarily shaped by government policies and funding programmes at a national scale.[39]

Further tensions exist between the adoption of a regional engagement mission and the increasing pressure on many institutions to be explicitly global facing in their competition for international students and positioning in world university rankings.[40] Hence, a persistent criticism of engaged university models is that they only partially and selectively reflect the actual drivers (e.g., marketization, research excellence) that are dominant in higher education systems.[41]

https://doi.org/10.1080/2578711X.2021.1891767

3.4 THE SYSTEM-BASED UNIVERSITY

One context in which subnational drivers can be seen to have encouraged university engagement is regional innovation policy. The development of these policies in the last 20 years has been informed by the non-linear and interactive understanding of knowledge production, dissemination and commercialization underlying regional (and national) innovation system frameworks.[42] As discussed in chapter 2, the distinctive research capabilities that universities possess mean they are often recognized as an integral element of regional innovation systems.

This model of a *system-based university* is therefore one defined by the HEI's embeddedness within this territorial environment, and its network relationships with other local innovation actors in the private and public sectors. In this sense, it shares ground with the model of an *entrepreneurial university* within the triple helix approach.

The centrality of universities to the innovation strategies of many regions means they are also in positions to exercise what has been called "system-level agency", that is, the ability to influence the evolving structures and priorities of the regional innovation system beyond their own organizational boundaries.[43] The system-based university therefore also overlaps with the developmental role of universities in regional governance and policy processes that is emphasized by *engaged university* models.

These functions of a system-based university can be illustrated with reference to the regional policy of the European Union, which supports research, technological development and innovation (RTDI) activities. Since the mid-1990s, the rationale for RTDI programmes in the Structural Funds has gradually shifted away from a linear model of investment in the "supply-side" research infrastructure towards policy interventions based on cultivating regional innovation systems.[44] In particular, these system-based approaches aim to increase the innovation capacities of less-favoured regions by stimulating demand for research and development amongst local businesses and strengthening their network links to sources of public and academic research capability.[45]

In the most recent Cohesion Policy period (2014–20), these goals were carried forward into the requirement for regions (or member states) across the European Union (EU) to develop Research and Innovation Strategies for Smart Specialisation (RIS3). The key step in preparing these strategies was the collective participation of local stakeholders in a bottom-up "entrepreneurial discovery process" (EDP) to identify opportunities for innovation-led growth or transformation in the regional economy that can be realized by concentrating funding for RTDI activities in specific domains.[46] Beyond the European Union, Smart Specialisation has also been advanced as a path towards innovation-driven growth for regions in Australia, Korea and Turkey by the OECD.[47]

With an EDP at its heart, Smart Specialisation is fundamentally a demand-side-focused approach to regional innovation policy. In practice, however, universities have played a number of important roles within the development and implementation of RIS3.[48] These include contributions to the supply of knowledge in regional innovation systems through their research activities, specialist training courses and engagements with local industry that are linked to the regional Smart Specialisation priorities.

Universities have also been core participants in the EDP in many regions. This intervention will have been especially important in those European regions where the conditionality of undertaking a comprehensive RIS3 process will have challenged the capacity for evidence-based policy and collaborative governance practices of the subnational government responsible for administrating the Structural Funds.[49]

For universities to perform this expanded developmental function within the EDP, it is necessary for them to be embedded within a regional innovation ecosystem of organizational interconnections.[50] Previous research has highlighted that the key dynamic at the heart of an RIS3, particularly in peripheral regions, can take the form of a cooperative strategic partnership between an HEI and local/regional authority with mutual understanding of the drivers and barriers on both sides.[51]

In many less developed regions, however, the misalignment between areas of academic research strength and regional economic needs, and the low absorptive capacity of the local business base (see chapter 2), will be significant barriers to universities contributing fully to the Smart Specialisation process.[52] To fulfil this role, therefore, it may require system-based universities to adapt their research activities to meet innovation priorities within their wider regional economy. This type of collective institutional change is, however, often difficult for university leaders to achieve due to internal factors within universities, including a decentralized organizational structure and weak incentives for academics to focus on new engagement activities with business in the region.[53]

3.5 CONCLUSIONS

This chapter has discussed three models of universities—*entrepreneurial*, *engaged* and *system based*—as institutional actors in regional development processes. As well as being developed as academic concepts, these models have shaped the more practice-oriented thinking of international organizations or networks, including MIT's REAP programme, the Triple Helix Association, the Talloires Network, OECD and the European Commission.

The chapter has also, however, highlighted the limitations of these models in terms of their application to less developed regional contexts, to higher education systems that do not incentivise regional engagement activities, and to organizational structures or cultures in universities that impede institution-wide adaptation to new strategic priorities.

These models, therefore, do not fully reflect the impact of diverse regional settings, policy environments (for higher education and territorial development), or management and organizational structures across different types of HEI. This raises questions about their relevance outside the universities, higher education systems and regional contexts where they were developed. As a result, there is a risk that their widespread adoption will lead to the design of policies that are not fit for purpose. The next chapter will therefore explore an alternative framework that aims to help regional policymakers and university leaders take these varied factors into account.

          https://doi.org/10.1080/2578711X.2021.1891767

NOTES

1. Youtie J and Shapira P (2008) Building an innovation hub: A case study of the transformation of university roles in regional technological and economic development. *Research Policy*, 37(8): 1118–1204.

2. Uyarra E (2010) Conceptualizing the regional roles of universities, implications and contradictions. *European Planning Studies*, 18(8): 1227–1246; Trippl M, Sinozic T and Lawton Smith H (2015) The role of universities in regional development: Conceptual models and policy institutions in the UK, Sweden and Austria. *European Planning Studies*, 23(9): 1722–1740.

3. Clark BR (1998) The entrepreneurial university: Demand and response. *Tertiary Education and Management*, 4(1): 5–16.

4. Nelles J and Vorley T (2010) Constructing an entrepreneurial architecture: An emergent framework for studying the contemporary university beyond the entrepreneurial turn. *Innovative Higher Education*, 35(3): 161–176.

5. Grimaldi R, Kenney M, Siegel DS and Wright M (2011) 30 years after Bayh–Dole: Reassessing academic entrepreneurship. *Research Policy*, 40(8): 1045–1057.

6. Mowery DC and Sampat BN (2005) The Bayh–Dole and university–industry technology transfer: A model for other OECD governments? *Journal of Technology Transfer*, 30(1–2): 115–127.

7. Olo D, Correia L and Rego MC (2020) The main challenges of higher education institutions in the 21st century: A focus on entrepreneurship. In AD Daniel, AAC Teixeira and MT Preto (eds.), *Examining the Role of Entrepreneurial Universities in Regional Development*, pp. 1–23. IGI Global. doi:10.4018/978-1-7998-0174-0.

8. Feldman MP (2000) Where science comes to life: University bioscience, commercial spin-offs, and regional economic development. *Journal of Comparative Policy Analysis: Research and Practice*, 2(3): 345–361.

9. Garnsey E and Heffernan P (2005) High-technology clustering through spin-out and attraction: The Cambridge case. *Regional Studies*, 39(8): 1127–1144.

10. Zucker LG and Darby MR (1996) Star scientists and institutional transformation: Patterns of invention and innovation in the formation of the biotechnology industry. *Proceedings of the National Academy of Sciences, USA*, 93(23): 12709–12716.

11. Benneworth P and Charles D (2005) University spin-off policies and economic development in less successful regions: Learning from two decades of policy practice. *European Planning Studies*, 13(4): 537–557.

12. Leslie SW and Kargon RH (1996) Selling Silicon Valley: Frederick Terman's model for regional advantage. *Business History Review*, 70(Winter): 435–472.

13. Piqué JM, Berbegal-Mirabent J and Etzkowitz H (2020) The role of universities in shaping the evolution of Silicon Valley's ecosystem of innovation. *Triple Helix Journal*. doi:10.1163/21971927-bja10009.

14. See https://reap.mit.edu/ [Accessed 20 July 2020].

15. Etzkowitz H, Webster A, Gebhardt C and Terra BRC (2000) The future of the university and the university of the future: Evolution of ivory tower to entrepreneurial paradigm. *Research Policy*, 29(2): 313–330.

16. Benneworth P, Lawton Smith H and Bagchi-Sen S (2015) Building inter-organizational synergies in the regional Triple Helix. *Industry and Higher Education*, 29(1): 5–10.

17. See https://www.triplehelixassociation.org/ [Accessed 20 July 2020].

[18] Gibb A A and Haskins G (2014) The university of the future: An entrepreneurial stakeholder learning organisation? In A Fayolle and DT Redford (eds.), *Handbook on the Entrepreneurial University*, pp. 25–63. Cheltenham: Edward Elgar.

[19] Abreu M, Grinevich V, Hughes A and Kitson M (2009) *Knowledge Exchange between Academics and the Business, Public and Third Sectors*. Cambridge: UK Innovation Research Centre.

[20] Uyarra E (2010) Conceptualizing the regional roles of universities, implications and contradictions. *European Planning Studies*, 18(8): 1227–1246.

[21] Sánchez-Barrioluengo M and Benneworth P (2019) Is the entrepreneurial university also regionally engaged? Analysing the influence of university's structural configuration on third mission performance. *Technological Forecasting and Social Change*, 141(April): 206–218; Bellandi M, Caloffi A and De Masi S (2020) Bottom-level organizational changes within entrepreneurial and engaged models of university: Insights from Italy. *Journal of Technology Transfer*. doi:10.1007/s10961-020-09805-6; Thomas E and Pugh R (2020) From "entrepreneurial" to "engaged" universities: Social innovation for regional development in the Global South. *Regional Studies*. doi:10. 1080/00343404.2020.1749586.

[22] Breznitz SM and Feldman MP (2012) The engaged university. *Journal of Technology Transfer*, 37(2): 139–157.

[23] Gunasekara C (2006) The generative and developmental roles of universities in regional innovation systems. *Science and Public Policy*, 33(2): 137–150.

[24] Goddard J and Vallance P (2013) *The University and the City*. London: Routledge.

[25] König A and Evans J (2013) Introduction: Experimenting for sustainable development? Living laboratories, social learning and the role of universities. In *Regenerative Sustainable Development of Universities and Cities: The Role of Living Laboratories*, pp. 1–24. Cheltenham: Edward Elgar; Tewdwr-Jones M (2017) Health, cities and planning: Using universities to achieve place innovation. *Perspectives in Public Health*, 137(1): 31–34; Van Geenhuizen M (2018) A framework for the evaluation of living labs as boundary spanners in innovation. *Environment and Planning C: Politics and Space*, 36(7): 1280–1298.

[26] Comunian R and Gilmore A (eds.) (2016) *Higher Education and the Creative Economy: Beyond the Campus*. Abingdon: Routledge.

[27] Chatterton P and Goddard J (2000) The response of higher education institutions to regional needs. *European Journal of Education*, 35(4): 475–496.

[28] Vallance P (2016) The historical roots and development of the civic university. In J Goddard, E Hazelkorn, L Kempton and P Vallance (eds.), *The Civic University: The Policy and Leadership Challenges*, pp. 16–33. Cheltenham: Edward Elgar.

[29] Sørensen M, Geschwind L, Kekäle J and Pinherio R (eds.) (2019) *The Responsible University: Exploring the Nordic Context and Beyond*. London: Palgrave Macmillan.

[30] Arocena R, Göransson B and Sutz J (2015) Knowledge policies and universities in developing countries: Inclusive development and the "developmental university". *Technology in Society*, 41(1): 10–20.

[31] Watson D, Hollister RM, Stroud SE and Babcock E (2011) *The Engaged University: International Perspectives on Civic Engagement*. London: Routledge.

[32] See https://talloiresnetwork.tufts.edu/ [Accessed 20 July 2020].

[33] Organisation for Economic Co-operation and Development (OECD) (2007) *Higher Education and Regions: Globally Competitive, Locally Engaged*. Paris: OECD.

[34] See https://www.oecd.org/education/imhe/highereducationinregionalandcitydevelopment.htm [Accessed 20 July 2020].

[35] Goddard J, Hazelkorn E, Kempton L and Vallance P (2016) Introduction: Why the civic university? In J Goddard, E Hazelkorn, L Kempton and P Vallance (eds.), *The Civic University: The Policy and Leadership Challenges*, pp. 3–15. Cheltenham: Edward Elgar.

[36] Goddard et al. (2016), see Reference 35.

[37] Goddard et al. (2016), see Reference 35.

[38] Hazelkorn E (2016) Contemporary debates. Part 2: Initiatives, governance and organisational structures. In J Goddard, E Hazelkorn, L Kempton and P Vallance (eds.), *The Civic University: The Policy and Leadership Challenges*, pp. 34–64. Cheltenham: Edward Elgar; Sánchez-Barrioluengo and Benneworth (2019), see Reference 21; Bellandi et al. (2020) , see Reference 21.

[39] Benneworth P, Zeeman N, Pinherio R and Karlsen J (2017) National higher education policies challenging universities' regional engagement activities. *Ekonomiaz*, 92(2): 112–139.

[40] Jöns H and Hoyler M (2013) Global geographies of higher education: The perspective of world university rankings. *Geoforum*, 46(1): 45–59; Hazelkorn E (2015) *Rankings and the Reshaping of Higher Education: The Battle for World-Class Excellence*. London: Palgrave Macmillan.

[41] Uyarra E (2010) Conceptualizing the regional roles of universities, implications and contradictions. *European Planning Studies*, 18(8): 1227–1246; Trippl et al. (2015) , see Reference 2.

[42] Asheim BT, Isaksen A and Trippl M (2020) The role of the regional innovation system approach in contemporary regional policy: Is it still relevant in a globalised world? In M González-López and BT Asheim (eds.), *Regions and Innovation Policies in Europe: Learning from the Margins*, pp. 1–11. Cheltenham: Edward Elgar.

[43] Isaksen A, Jakobsen S-E, Njøs R and Normann R (2019) Regional industrial restructuring resulting from individual and system agency. *European Journal of Social Science Research*, 32(1): 48–65.

[44] Morgan K and Nauwelaers C (1999) A regional perspective on innovation: From theory to strategy. In K Morgan and C Nauwelaers (eds.), *Regional Innovation Strategies: The Challenge for Less Favoured Regions*, pp. 1–17. London: Routledge; Musyck B and Reid A (2007) Innovation and regional development: Do European Structural Funds make a difference? *European Planning Studies*, 15(7): 961–983.

[45] Oughton C, Landabaso M and Morgan K (2002) The regional innovation paradox: Innovation policy and industrial policy. *Journal of Technology Transfer*, 27(1): 97–110.

[46] Foray D (2015) *Smart Specialisation: Opportunities and Challenges for Regional Innovation Policy*. Abingdon: Routledge.

[47] Organisation for Economic Co-operation and Development (OECD) (2013) *Innovation-Driven Growth in Regions: The Role of Smart Specialisation*. Paris: OECD.

[48] Vallance P, Blažek J, Edwards J and Květoň V (2018) Smart Specialisation in regions with less-developed research and innovation systems: A changing role for universities? *Environment and Planning C: Politics and Space*, 36(2): 219–238.

[49] Muscio A, Reid A and Rivera Leon L (2015) A empirical test of the regional innovation paradox: Can Smart Specialisation overcome the paradox in Central and Eastern Europe? *Journal of Economic Policy Reform*, 18(2): 153–171; Morgan K (2017) Nurturing novelty: Regional innovation policy in the age of Smart Specialisation. *Environment and Planning C: Politics and Space*, 35(4): 569–583.

50 Markkula M and Kune H (2015) Making smart regions smarter: Smart Specialization and the role of universities in regional innovation ecosystems. *Technology Innovation Management Review*, 5(10): 7–15; Virkkala S, Mäenpää A and Mariussen Å (2017) A connectivity model as a potential tool for Smart Specialization strategies. *European Planning Studies*, 25(4): 661–679.

51 Kempton L (2015) Delivering Smart Specialization in peripheral regions: The role of universities. *Regional Studies, Regional Science*, 2(1): 489–496; Edwards J, Marinelli E, Arregui-Pabollet E and Kempton L (2017) *Higher education for Smart Specialisation: Towards strategic partnerships for innovation* (S3 Policy Brief Series No. 23/2017). Brussels: European Commission.

52 Marques P and Morgan K (2018) The heroic assumptions of Smart Specialisation: A sympathetic critique of regional innovation policy. In A Isaksen, R Martin and M Trippl (eds.), *New Avenues for Regional Innovation Systems— Theoretical Advances, Empirical Cases and Policy Lessons*, pp. 275–293. New York: Springer.

53 Benneworth P, Pinheiro R and Karlsen J (2017b) Strategic agency and institutional change: Investigating the role of universities in regional innovation systems (RISs). *Regional Studies*, 51(2): 235–248.

https://doi.org/10.1080/2578711X.2021.1891767

4. PLACING UNIVERSITIES AND REGIONAL RELATIONSHIPS IN CONTEXT

Keywords: regional knowledge, territorial engagement, helix model, civic university

4.1 INTRODUCTION

From a global perspective, higher education institution (HEIs) contribute to regional development through different ways, depending on the local or national context, policy frameworks, and institutional leadership.

Based on the potential effects that HEIs have on the surroundings, many regional political leaders identify these institutions as the panacea to resolve local and regional development problems. However, even though we are already far from the classical portrayal of HEIs as an "ivory tower", it is not possible that the development process of a territory is only related to the existence of HEIs in their regions:

> *The existence, or even the creation, of universities does not, in itself, guarantee regional economic growth since the transfer of knowledge and the generation of innovations are not automatic and much less immediate.*[1]

The limits (or barriers) to the regional effects of HEIs, in general, may be related to factors that concern the HEIs themselves or other local and regional stakeholders and how the territorial ecosystem is structured.[2]

Therefore, it is essential to discuss how HEIs, together with stakeholders, can implement effective cooperation processes that promote higher levels of knowledge, competitiveness, cohesion and quality of life. In this respect, the European Commission has recommended a focus on the "regional knowledge triangle", which combines research, education and innovation (Figure 4.1).[3]

In the contemporary economy, innovation is deemed to be the major driver of economic growth, and the stock of talented people and skilled human capital is a key factor in regions' socioeconomic development.

In line with this point of view, four ways have been identified[4] in which universities could create activities globally, focused on knowledge and local engagement and innovation, by:

Figure 4.1 Regional knowledge triangle.

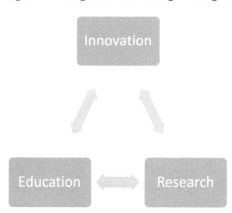

Source: Author after the European Commission.

- supporting new enterprises and their emergence with labour market up-skilling;

- developing and attracting world-class academics who may contribute to regional innovation networks in their host regions;

- creating structures to steer and support academics towards regional engagement; and

- raising the regional innovation strategy processes and quality by helping to create collective innovation assets.

https://doi.org/10.1080/2578711X.2021.1891768

These perspectives stress the importance of human capital in the performance of regions. The role of both HEIs and companies in attracting and retaining students and highly qualified professionals is crucial in the framework of regional innovation performance.[5]

Graduates are truly relevant to a region's development process insofar as stakeholders absorb them in order to promote a better knowledge transference. Additionally, there is also the link between cutting-edge research and its regional application.[6] In the context of regional involvement, the cooperation between university and industry should privilege small to medium-sized businesses and regional value chains, and adapt the knowledge transferred to the needs of local stakeholders. In this sense, besides the absorptive capacity in companies, it is fundamental that researchers are motivated to do this.

4.2 DOMAINS OF TERRITORIAL ENGAGEMENT

Regions are naturally different, the consequence of their physical/geographical conditions (relief, climate, hydrography, vegetation, the potential of natural resources, economic occupation, available labour, infrastructure). These factors stimulate or interrupt the regional development process, occurring spontaneously or induced through elements that are endogenous (internal) or exogenous (external) to the regional territory.

Other internal elements that are reflected in regional dynamics are the resistance of the physical or social environment with respect to changes, whether this is the result of environmental issues, religious beliefs or political cultures, and even the availability and transparency of intelligence and information, impacting upon the capacity for innovation, change and the absorption of knowledge, new technologies, and regulatory action of the institutions of government.

The exogenous elements (external to the region) refer to interventions to improve the profile of regional development or in a specific sector, mainly by the public sector, but they can also come from the private sector. These interventions can, for example, improve the regional physical infrastructure, policy context, governance or the quality of life itself, and can enhance the attractiveness (or otherwise) of the region for new investment, increasing local potential, strengthening the profitability of investments, and social and institutional innovation.[7]

It is in this regional context, with internal and external differences, that HEIs are located. Just as cities and regions are heterogeneous, having different dynamics in terms of size, function, and relative territorial position and hierarchy, HEIs also present different engagements and impacts as they may "use" and will be "used" in different ways by regions.

HEIs are complex organizations with specific traditions, diverse cultural heritage, distinct hierarchical decision-making and heterogeneous interest-representation structures. As discussed in previous chapters, in recent years several attempts have been made to create conceptual frameworks and models to help universities and policymakers to understand the role and contribution of HEIs to local and regional development. But these models have failed to fully reflect (or give insufficient attention to):

- the impact of the regional context (economic, social, political);
- the policy environment for higher education and territorial development; and
- the diversity of management and leadership structures of universities themselves.

The core of domains in the relationship between HEIs and the place where they are located is illustrated in Figure 4.2. It relates the internal context of HEIs (institutional characteristics) with the external environment (governance of regional development, national and regional policy context, and characteristics of place).

Depending on the characteristics of these domains and the nature of their relationships, the territorial effects of HEIs:

- bring different types of institutional linkages, which could be anchored (embedded) or, on the other side, radical (disruptive); and
- give rise to different HEIs contributions, which can be isolated and without much relational density (providing ad hoc intelligence) or strongly linked (providing strategic leadership).

Figure 4.2 Domains for territorial engagement considering institutional and local contexts specificities

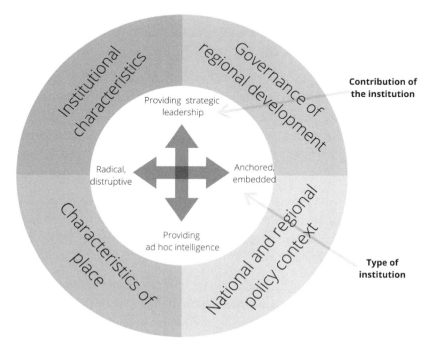

https://doi.org/10.1080/2578711X.2021.1891768

The interactions between HEIs and regions depend on the HEI's performance, the relationship they develop with their surroundings, and their characteristics, including the regions' historical legacy.[8] In each case, the dynamics of the regional ecosystems will be more as promoters of development, change and well-being in the region, features that are linked well to concept of the civic university.

A civic university is an HEI that possesses a place-based approach to link the activities of the university to its surroundings; the concept highlights and acknowledges the fact that HEIs can have a number of interlinkages with their environment and place through interaction with the research and policy communities, and the development of development projects such science parks, university hospitals and creative or cultural quarters.[9]

In this respect, because universities can have multiple and different links with the place and institutions in their vicinity, the phrase "one size doesn't fit all" might be the best way to describe the range of interactions present: "Universities are more likely to be actors involved over multiple scales; they are global players who are highly influential beyond their immediate locale while exhibiting a significant capacity to affect the social, spatial, and symbolic structures."[10]

Geographical proximity is also an important feature when analysing the role of HEIs. The literature has shown that the greater the distance, the lesser the effects of the HEI in that region. Several reasons may explain this factor. The demand for universities tends to be higher among the resident population surrounding the university, which diminishes in strength as one moves away from the specific location of the HEI.

This proximity issue may be due to personal preferences, aptitudes, or socioeconomic conditions, as distance will normally increase the financial and personal costs of attending higher education. This is particularly the case for less favoured socioeconomic groups and regions in terms of both the demand for and supply of higher education.[11]

Likewise, the positive results of the direct and multiplier effects of income and employment, and the use of qualified labour and the overflow of research, tend to be greater the closer they are to HEIs. For this reason, several initiatives have emerged in nations to achieve a spatially balanced HEI network. This is not only for equitable purposes but also as a deliberate political tool to achieve regional cohesion, and is evident in parts of Northern Europe and in South America.[12] In Brazil, for example, affirmative action for higher education has sought to reduce social and racial inequalities in regions (Box 4.1).

Regions with dynamic and more consolidated productive structures tend to have a regional system of innovation either present or in formation. In these regions, HEIs play a central role as they can carry out research and development (R&D) and interact locally from their teaching, research and entrepreneurship missions. As a consequence, universities' strategies and policies often change to adapt to this external need as the academy interacts with the productive sector.

Universities often seek to stimulate these processes through the creation of industrial liaison offices (ILOs), technology licensing offices (TLOs) or innovation and technology centres (NITs). However, as has been pointed out, HEIs do not need to interact only with the provision of technologies in their strict sense.[13] They

Box 4.1 Addressing social and racial inequality through higher education

In Brazil, the right to education is enshrined in the Federal Constitution of 1988, granted for its relevance in the process of education and instruction of citizens. However, in relation to higher education, regional asymmetries, racial, social and religious differences, and problems related to class inequalities, have forced the country to adopt measures to universalize access to higher education.

Called "Affirmative Policies" or "Affirmative Actions", they are aimed at democratizing access to universities, especially state and federal public universities, in order to promote equal opportunities. The intention is to facilitate access for high-school graduates and low-income youth and, in parallel, access for young brown, black and indigenous peoples, and those with disabilities:

> the Brazilian government has structured, since 2007, a more general movement for reform and expansion of higher education, based on the Education Development Plan (PDE), whose main universal policy for higher education is the Program to Support Federal University Restructuring and Expansion Plans (Reuni). However, although Reuni organized and modulated public policies for higher education, a focused affirmative action policy had been created before it aimed at facilitating participation in higher education for low-income, disabled and/or young people from schools public: ProUni, focused on private higher education, was created by Law N° 11,096 of January 13, 2005, offering scholarships in courses from private institutions. On the other hand, after Reuni, a public policy focused on a broader scope than previous reparatory actions was created: the Quota Program, focusing on public higher education, was created by Law N° 12,711 of August 2012, with the objective of expand the access of the lower classes to federal universities and federal institutes of education.[14]

Under the Quota Law, at least 50% of university places are offered to students who have completed high school in public schools. Of this percentage, 50% is reserved for students from families with an income equal to or less than the minimum wage plus a half. Also, places are reserved for self-declared blacks, browns, indigenous people and those with disabilities in the population of the state where the university is located, according to the census of the Brazilian Institute of Geography and Statistics (IBGE). The remainder of the places, the other 50%, are for non-quota holders, that is, those who make the selection process in wide competition, which do not fit the above criteria.

The federal government delegates to affirmative action policies, a central role in combating inequality in higher education, taking a proactive stance on the issue of exclusion. This policy does not solve the whole problem, and there remain issues of young people starting from different points when competing for places. But it is a commendable action for countries with such pronounced racial and social inequality.[15]

can promote collective learning and communication processes, social and non-technological networks, and of course trust.

In peripheral regions, or those regions lacking a regional innovation system, the main contribution of HEIs in and to a region is enhancing the qualifications of local students, encouraging new ideas and enhancing the intellectual capacity of communities.

https://doi.org/10.1080/2578711X.2021.1891768

These are not in themselves insubstantial contributions, but some universities manage to go much further in their regional contributions. The ability of HEIs to go that extra distance is largely dependent on their local conditions:

> *Entrepreneurial ecosystems do not emerge just anywhere. They need fertile soil … entrepreneurial ecosystems have typically emerged in places that already have an established and highly regarded knowledge base which employs significant numbers of scientists and engineers. These organisations are the source of the skilled personnel who start businesses. These knowledge institutions—research universities, public research laboratories and corporate R&D labs—perform several roles in seeding the cluster.[16]*

The traditional functions of HEIs—teaching and research—are in themselves essential for this more entrepreneurial possibility. But universities need to accelerate their regional intervention if they are to become more progressive and active agents of change in their own places. This would include, for example, stimulating their local engagement, getting involved with their immediate neighbourhoods, transferring knowledge, participating in discussions with a range of sectors, and influencing and informing the development of new policies and new economic initiatives.

As a result of pursuing these accelerated forms of regional interaction, universities will be much more closely aligned to the productive sector, able to offer assistance to local companies, active in the political discussions of development choices with local, subnational and national governments, and become actively involved with local communities.[17] Box 4.2 outlines a case study university that has gone on to accelerate its regional role.

The interactions described above are part of the Regional Innovation Systems (RIS) framework. RIS, aligned to the regions' characteristics and needs, are potentially effective instruments in improving competitiveness and wealth creation. Box 4.3 presents the case of an RIS in the peripheral Portuguese region of Alentejo.

The RIS development is in line with what is theoretically recommended by a "triple helix" concept. The knowledge-based region is a consciously built entity structured by several actors, including a triple helix of government, industry and university as its engine.[18] Based on the triple helix framework, the regional advantage is intrinsically related to the endogenous capacity for knowledge creation and exploitation. Its construction depends on several factors, ranging from governance systems and knowledge bases to a better interaction between the public and private sectors.

However, it is worth stressing that the interplay between the actors of the triple helix[19] assumes particular importance insomuch as it is essential for promoting regional economic activities:

- the university plays a pivotal role through knowledge production under distinct ways; it forms highly skilled human capital, promoting the processes of technology transfer, and sets up science and technology parks and incubators, which may lead to generating spin-off companies; and

> **Box 4.2 Developing entrepreneurial capacity: a case study of the Federal University of Pará (UFPA), Brazil**
>
> The UFPA is a university located in a developing country (Brazil), and in a peripheral Brazilian region. The state of Pará is rich in natural and mineral resources and multi-ethnic, but it is marked by the existence of a discontinuous and low-density urban network in a state of vast territorial dimension (the size of Spain, France, Portugal and Iceland added together). The region has serious social and economic vulnerabilities, and limited and fragile university–business relationships. However, UFPA has also become a case study reference HEI in Brazil. Even in a region with so many difficulties in developing a regional innovation system, UFPA has carried out its teaching and research missions and has intensified its regional engagement.
>
> UFPA decided to participate in the National Training Plan for Basic Education Teachers (Parfor), proposed by the Coordination for the Improvement of Higher Education Personnel (Capes), which aims to minimize the problems of the low level of teaching qualifications in the basic education network of many regions of Brazil, mirrored in Pará state. Just 10% of teachers had adequate initial qualifications, and the other 90% either did not have higher education experience or, if they did, they did not work in their area of formation.
>
> It was in this context that UFPA accepted the challenge of trying to change these statistics by signing a Term of Adhesion to the Technical Cooperation Agreement with Capes and the State Education Secretariat of Pará for 2009–15.
>
> In the following years, research showed a significant improvement in the rates of basic education in the municipalities of Pará, where UFPA had achieved some influence either directly or indirectly, and increased the number and quality of teachers with basic-level qualifications. UFPA's participation was so important and significant that in 2015 there were already 60 teacher-training centres formed across Pará state.
>
> The university has since consolidated itself as a strategic actor in government policies. Overall, UFPA's participation in educational strategies for the basic level may further cause the development of a viable and consolidated structured innovation system from Pará as a whole.[20]

- the companies and public organizations must correspond to this interaction through the absorption and integration of innovative knowledge, the retention and attraction of graduates, and the communication to HEIs of innovation and technology needs.

Following the evolution of social challenges, the triple helix framework has evolved into a new matrix that also includes civil society, named the quadruple helix,[21] and more recently a quintuple helix,[22] which includes the natural environment (Figure 4.3).

The helix model appears as a theoretical framework for the transdisciplinary analysis of sustainable development and social ecology. With this concept, we can understand the evolution of the nature of the relationships established between all regional stakeholders in the relevant domains at each historical moment, highlighting HEIs' pivotal effect in relation to other regional institutions. It has a strong potential to accompany and accommodate the evolution of societal concerns over time and, in relation to them, set out an articulated community interaction.

https://doi.org/10.1080/2578711X.2021.1891768

Box 4.3   A Regional Innovation System (RIS) in a European peripheral region

Alentejo is the largest Portuguese region (NUTS-II), occupying one-third of the area of the mainland; it is located in the centre-south of the country and has about 5% of the Portuguese population. Alentejo is a convergence region (with a gross domestic product (GDP) per capita < 75% of the EU-28 average).

The regional economic activity—based primarily on services and non-tradable goods—creates low-income levels: Alentejo is a traditionally large-estate (*latifúndio*) agricultural region with heavily rented landowners. It faces a "vicious cycle of low density", whereby the effects of a shrinking and ageing population and declining economic activity are compounded and perpetuated.

Évora, a small to medium-sized town, is the largest in Alentejo (with about 50,000 inhabitants), where the main regional public services are located. The predominant sector in the city is tertiary, with an emphasis on trade, public administration, tourism and education. The city has a diverse range of small companies and some multinationals manufacturing electronic components and parts for the aircraft industry. Évora is also known for its culture and heritage (the United Nations Educational, Scientific and Cultural Organization (UNESCO) classified its historic city centre in 1986 as a World Heritage Site).

Within the framework of European Union structural policy, a set of diverse regional entities promoted the Regional System of Technology Transfer of Alentejo (RSTTA). RSTTA embeds the concept of the value network, based on the development and qualification of regional competences, reinforced by market-oriented national and international networks, and focused on the development of innovative goods and services that promote the region through the improvement of its entrepreneurial dynamics.

RSTTA is organized into five components: The Alentejo Science and Technology Park (PACT),[23] and four subsystems (technological incubators, scientific and technological infrastructures, infrastructures with high synergetic potential, and technological and industrial parks and areas). RSTTA is grounded on PACT's roles as a focal point and a provider of leverage for the other subsystems. The park is the central infrastructure of the RSTTA; it is also the region's primary incubator for technology development, fostering the environment required for accelerating the commercialization of research and to support innovation and entrepreneurship.

PACT focuses on diverse themes and competences, which are critical for developing regional innovation and competitiveness, namely: energy and mobility, mechatronics, information and communication technologies, food and agricultural technologies, materials, biotechnology, and environment/sustainability.

PACT is located in Évora's industrial park and has access to the resources of its cluster of leading HEIs: the polytechnic institutes of Beja, Santarém and Portalegre and the University of Évora, its principal shareholder. It started its activity in 2011 to create and develop companies in Alentejo, promoting scientific capacity, encouraging knowledge transfer for this region, and becoming a pole of attraction for innovative companies with sustainable results.

PACT's mission is defined as: (1) boosting the creation and growth of companies in Alentejo; (2) creating an innovation ecosystem, attracting innovative companies with sustainable results; (3) promoting Alentejo's scientific capacity and international ambition; and (4) contributing to an innovation agenda, encouraging the transfer of knowledge between the research base (universities, polytechnics and the state) and innovative companies.[24]

Figure 4.3 Knowledge production and innovation.[25]

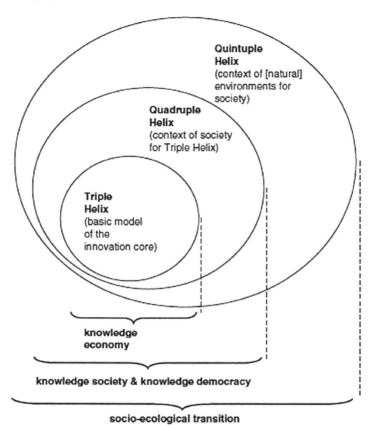

Another dimension to the role of the university in the region is related to the main funding source: HEIs can be either public or private, since that will allow or limit their ability to respond to regional issues in different ways, and this might vary greatly, country to country.

The public HEIs can be supported by governments, religious organizations, other non-profit institutions, or can operate as collaborations with local and international institutions. The private HEIs are institutions that aim for profit. This is important to consider because a university's overall mission might be to proceed for private value rather than as a public good. However, the distinction is more blurred than it used to be. Actually, even public HEIs can operate as businesses in a globally competitive market for students and research funding.

HEIs, whether public or private, can therefore differ in terms of accountability, budgeting, ownership and overarching goals. Human resource systems in public organizations tend to be merit based, and performance incentives tend to be lower than the private sector. According to the literature, public HEIs are more open to environmental (i.e., contextual) influences as a result of their accountability to multiple constituencies, policymakers and legislative mandates.[26]

https://doi.org/10.1080/2578711X.2021.1891768

4.3 CONDITIONS FOR TERRITORIAL ENGAGEMENT

The connection between the presence of an HEI and regional prosperity is neither automatic nor deterministic, since there are several constraints. Besides the impact on regional income and the improvement of competitiveness, related to the supply-side effects of HEIs, cooperation can contribute to territorial cohesion. This domain includes the contribution to social, cultural and environmental development through formal and informal participation in regional networks of learning, innovation and governance.[27]

The perspective of a "civic university" implies a greater, and mutual, alignment between the higher education functions and regional development trajectories. This challenges the traditional idea of universities, as institutions that promote not only entrepreneurship and innovation but also integration and socialization.[28]

Given the potentialities, and the constraints, of cooperation between HEIs and local stakeholders, it is important to discuss the determinants that shape this interaction.

The characteristics and level of competition of universities, and the characteristics of regions, can all determine interaction:

- Newer universities and those located in peripheral regions tend to maintain more substantial cooperation levels with the community: "Universities that are comprehensively engaged in their region's development tend to be single relatively large scale universities located in peripheral regions."[29]

- New or modern universities, more geographically disperse, tend to prioritize local development, more so than older universities.

- Traditional HEIs tend to be more concerned with their position in higher education rankings.

The activities conducted also depend on the characteristics of the regions, once the contributions to social life or, globally, community engagement are more common in peripheral areas. One of the main determinants for HEIs' regional involvement is the motivation of their teachers and researchers. The possibility of finding funding in these regional surroundings often stimulates the decision whether or not to cooperate:

Small, teaching oriented universities and, in the German case, universities of applied science are key to the emergence of local pools and networks,[30]

which reflects the important role of so-called "mid-range universities".

The implementation of regional cooperation processes is just one of the tasks in which university staff can be involved, but these take their place alongside traditional research and teaching roles. Studies have highlighted frequent internal conflicts within HEIs between the pursuit of excellence activities in teaching and in research (which can be often associated with increasing the institution's prestige and reputation in national and international terms), and commitments to and time for regional engagement.[31]

Traditional academic values within universities have, historically, given little weight for staff to engage with local communities; HEIs offer limited incentives or resources to pursue an activity that serves the region. The scope of internal institutional acknowledgements (e.g., through incentives, rewards and promotion criteria) is important in stimulating and incentivizing academics to engage and cooperate with stakeholders.[32] As cooperation activities are less valued and associated with lower levels of international and national reputation, albeit may generate significant local and regional impacts, it will always be a second choice for some teachers and researchers. It is not only individual staff that this applies to.

Regional engagement must be clearly part of the institution's strategy, recognized at all levels and divisions internally, if a wider set of values and missions are to emerge. The autonomy of HEIs to make decisions in this respect is fundamental.

However, there remain challenges between the autonomy of individual teachers and researchers to embark on regional engagement, and possibly contrasting attitudes and values of senior managers in universities who may reiterate alternative priorities.

In regional cooperation, the participation of industry or policy organizations is essential. The construction of good communication mechanisms between HEIs and companies or governments should make it possible to blur barriers in order to enhance HEIs' knowledge missions. In addition, knowing about the absorptive capacity allows the process to be effective: on the one hand, the knowledge transferred must correspond to needs and, on the other, external organizations must identify and convey their needs to universities.

For industrial partners, what are the reasons why firms wish to collaborate with local HEIs? According to some,[33] there are proximity benefits, confidence, reputation and the goal of building a more prosperous region. In fact, the knowledge transference cost increases with distance and collaborating locally reduces the risk of information loss. Face-to-face contact helps to transfer knowledge and engender trust; if the local HEI can make a useful contribution, satisfying the requirements of external agencies, companies may see collaboration as a long-term investment, helping to build regional research quality to benefit future development while contributing to the community.

Leadership, and the implementation of regional development and education policies, particularly higher education policy, can also be key determinants of cooperation.

The ability of HEIs to become regional leaders assumes that: "they act not only as educators but also as institutional entrepreneurs, proactively networking, shaping regional strategies and attempting to change local routines as well as national policies."[34]

The regionalization of the higher education system, regional identity and networks is among factors that can foster or hinder the HEIs' regional engagement. More active regional engagement can be constrained (or even promoted) by the orientation of public policy, funding and incentives, decisions of leadership within HEIs, and the capacity of local and regional agents to get involved with higher education.

Regional engagement strategies of HEIs depend on the role the HEI chooses for itself and the leadership role it adopts. The options about governance, leadership and management of HEIs define the scope of active regional engagement, since—as we know—leadership and management styles vary by person and by sector.

In order to improve the regional commitment of HEIs, some public policy measures can directly relate to HEIs, as well as their relation to the environment (Box 4.4).[35] Many of these requirements coalesce around calls to increase funding for higher education specifically to resource the costs of regional engagement.

There are critical drivers of change for better regional commitment. Table 4.1 presents these drivers by building on the framework (Figure 4.2) outlined previously. What matters really is the character of the place, the region's spirit of authenticity and the common purpose shared by all regional stakeholders, including HEIs.[37]

Successful regions rely, in part, upon a dynamic interplay between actors who engage in sharing knowledge and expertise, which encourages a cooperative spirit and environment.

Table 4.1 Drivers for better regional engagement (commitment)

Institutional characteristics	Governance of regional development	National and regional policy context	Characteristics of place
Recognize and valorize local engagement in the academic *milieu*	Decentralize the decision-making by political, local and regional institutions	Build place-based policies in the domain of regional development as in the higher education field	Explore the characteristics/specificities of place, strengthening capacity-building

Source: Author.

The contribution of higher education to regional development can be successful if it is based on the distinct characteristics of regional ecosystems and the diversity and heterogeneity of HEIs, enhancing a higher education policy with local characteristics. This, in turn, fosters a *place-based* higher education policy.

4.4 CONCLUSIONS

This chapter has discussed the context for universities and their regional relationships. HEIs' contributions to regional development depend on a large set of characteristics from local and national contexts, policy frameworks, institutional leadership and positioning in relation to the place where they are located.

The domains in the relationship between HEIs and their surroundings are described and discussed, setting out the diversity resulting from the articulation of the internal characteristics of HEIs with the external environments. These differences are illustrated through cases analysed in several geographical contexts. The determinants of the territorial engagement presented shows that HEIs and regions evolve into different levels of commitment due to the characteristics of HEIs and the institutions or companies with whom they interact.

In the next chapter presents a new ORPHIC Framework for universities and regional contributions that strengthens the role of universities in their place.

NOTES

[1] Serra M, Rolim C and Bastos AP (2018) Universidades e a "mão invisível" do desenvolvimento regional. In M Serra, C Rolim and AP Bastos (eds.), *Universidades e Desenvolvimento Regional—as bases para a inovação competitive*, pp 31–52. Rio de Janeiro: Ideia D, at 39.

[2] Kempton L (2018) Solução milagrosa ou o ouro dos tolos? O papel das universidades nos sistemas regionais de inovação. In M Serra, C Rolim and AP Bastos (eds.), *Universidades e Desenvolvimento Regional—as bases para a inovação competitiva*. Rio de Janeiro: Ideia D: 53–82.

[3] See https://ec.europa.eu/transparency/regexpert/index.cfm?do=groupDetail.groupDetailDoc&id=28229&no=5 [Accessed 1 March 2020].

[4] Benneworth P and Dahl Fitjar R (2019) Contextualizing the role of universities to regional development. *Regional Studies, Regional Science*, 6(1): 331–338. doi:10.1080/21681376.2019.1601593.

[5] Uyarra E (2010) Conceptualizing the regional roles of universities, implications and contradictions. *European Planning Studies*, 18(8): 1227–1246. doi:10.1080/09654311003791275.

[6] Benneworth and Fitjar (2019), see Reference 4.

[7] Ferrera de Lima J (2016) O espaço e a difusão do desenvolvimento econômico regional. In CA Piacenti, J Ferrera de Lima and PHC Eberhardt (eds.), *Economia e desenvolvimento regional*, pp 15–40. Foz do Iguaçu: Parque Itaipu;

https://doi.org/10.1080/2578711X.2021.1891768

Alves LR (2016) Região, urbanização e polarização. In CA Piacenti, J Ferrera de Lima and PHC Eberhardt (eds.), *Economia e desenvolvimento regional*, pp 41–52. Foz do Iguaçu: Parque Itaipu.

[8] Pinheiro R, Benneworth P and Jones GA (2012) *Universities and Regional Development: A Critical Assessment of Tensions and Contradictions*. New York: Routledge, Taylor & Francis.

[9] OECD (2007) *Higher education and regions: Globally competitive, locally engaged*. Paris: OECD.

[10] Addie J-PD, Keil R and Olds K (2015) Beyond town and gown: Universities, territoriality and the mobilization of New Urban structures in Canada. *Territory, Politics, Governance*, 3: 27–50, at 30. doi:10.1080/21622671.2014.924 875.

[11] Vieira C, Vieira I and Raposo L (2017) Distance and academic performance in higher education. *Spatial Economic Analysis*, 13(1): 60–79. doi:10.1080/17421772.2017.1369146; Fitjar RD and Gjelsvik M (2018) Why do firms collaborate with local universities? *Regional Studies*, 52(11): 1525–1536. doi:10.1080/00343404.201 7.1413237.

[12] Dalmarco G, Hulsink W and Blois G (2018) Creating entrepreneurial universities in an emerging economy: Evidence from Brazil. *Technological Forecasting and Social Change*, 135: 99–111. doi:10.1016/j.techfore.2018.04.015.

[13] Mello Neto, RD, Medeiros HAV, Paiva FS, and Simões JL (2014) O impacto do Enem nas políticas de democratização do acesso ao Ensino superior brasileiro. *Comunicações*, 21(3): 109–123, at 113.

[14] Gianezini K and Rodrigues AB (2019) *Políticas públicas no século XXI*. Criciúma: UNESC; Morais DMG, Junger AP, Zambra EM, Facó JFB and Bresciani LP (2020) A evolução do ensino superior brasileiro na perspectiva do desenvolvimento regional. *Research, Society and Development*, 9(3). https://doi.org/10.33448/rsd-v9i3.2264.

[15] Kitagawa F (2004) Universities and regional advantage: Higher education and innovation policies in English regions. *European Planning Studies*, 12(6): 835–852. doi:10.1080/0965431042000251882.

[16] Mason C and Brown R (2014) *Entrepreneurial Ecosystems and Growth Oriented Entrepreneurship*. Background paper prepared for the workshop organised by the OECD LEED Programme and the Dutch Ministry of Economic Affairs, The Hague, the Netherlands, at 13. Available at: https://www.oecd.org/cfe/leed/Entrepreneurial-ecosystems.pdf

[17] Aranguren MJ and Magro E (2020) How can universities contribute to regional competitiveness policy-making? *Competitiveness Review*, 30(2): 101–11. doi:10.1108/CR-11-2018-0071.

[18] Etzkowitz H, Ranga M, Benner M, Guaranys L, Maculan AM and Kneller R, (2008) Pathways to the entrepreneurial university: Towards a global convergence. *Science and Public Policy*, 35(9): 681–695.

[19] Etzkowitz H (2008) *The Triple Helix: University–Industry–Government Innovation in Action*. London: Routledge. https://doi.org/10.3152/030234208X389701.

[20] Serra et al. (2018), see Reference 1.

[21] Liljemark T (2004) *Innovation Policy in Canada: Strategy and Realities*. Stockholm: Swedish Institute for Growth Policy Studies; Van Horne C and Dutot V (2016) Challenges in technology transfer: An actor perspective in a quadruple helix environment. *Journal of Technology Transfer*, 42(2): 1–17.

[22] Carayannis EG and Campbell DFJ (2011) Open innovation diplomacy and a 21st century fractal research, education and innovation (FREIE) ecosystem: Building on the quadruple and quintuple helix innovation concepts and the "Mode 3" knowledge production system. *Journal of the Knowledge Economy*, 2(3): 327–372; Carayannis EG and Rakhmatullin R (2014) The quadruple/quintuple innovation helixes and Smart Specialisation strategies for sustainable and inclusive growth in Europe and beyond. *Journal of Knowledge Economy*, 5(2): 212–239; Kolehmainen J,

Irvine J, Stewart L, Karacsonyi Z, Szabó T, Alarinta J and Norberg A (2016) Quadruple helix, innovation and the knowledge-based development: Lessons from remote, rural and less-favoured regions. *Journal of the Knowledge Economy*, 7(1): 23–42.

[23] See https://www.pact.pt/site/sobre/.

[24] Lucas MR, Rego MC, Vieira C and Vieira I (2017) Proximity and cooperation for innovative regional development: The case of the Science and Technology Park of Alentejo. In L Carvalho (ed.), *Handbook of Research on Entrepreneurial Development and Innovation within Smart Cities*, pp. 208–238. Hershey: IGI Global. doi:10.4018/978-1-5225-1978-2.

[25] Carayannis E, Barth TD and Campbell DFJ (2012) The quintuple helix innovation model: Global warming as a challenge and drivers for innovation. *Journal of Innovation and Entrepreneurship*, 1: art. 2, at 4. doi:10.1186/2192-5372-1-2.

[26] Carayannis et al. (2012), see Reference 25.

[27] Uyarra (2010), see Reference 5.

[28] Benneworth P (2013) The engaged university in practice? Reinventing the social compact for the grand societal challenges. In P Benneworth (ed.), *University Engagement with Socially Excluded Communities*, pp. 329–343. Dordrecht: Springer. doi:10.1007/978-94-007-4875-0.

[29] Boucher G, Conway C and Van der Meer E (2003) Tiers of engagement by universities in their region's development. *Regional Studies*, 37(9): 887–897, at 895. doi:10.1080/0034340032000143896.

[30] Kroll H, Dornbusch F and Schnabl E (2016) Universities' regional involvement in Germany: How academics' objectives and opportunity shape choices of activity. *Regional Studies*, 50(9): 1595–1610, at 1606. doi:10.1080/00343404.2015.1051016.

[31] Uyarra (2010), see Reference 5; Kempton (2018), see Reference 2.

[32] Organisation for Economic Co-operation and Development (OECD) (2007) *Higher Education and Regions: Globally Competitive, Locally Engaged*. Paris: OECD; Kempton (2018), see Reference 2.

[33] Fitjar RD and Gjelsvik M (2018) Why do firms collaborate with local universities? *Regional Studies*, 52(11): 1525–1536. doi:10.1080/00343404.2017.1413237.

[34] Raagmaa G and Keerberg A (2017) Regional higher education institutions in regional leadership and development. *Regional Studies*, 51(2): 260–272, at 270. doi:10.1080/00343404.2016.1215600.

[35] Benneworth P and Charles D (2013) University–community engagement in the wider policy environment. In P Benneworth (ed.), *University Engagement with Socially Excluded Communities*, pp. 223–241. Dordrecht: Springer. doi:10.1007/978-94-007-4875-0.

[36] Benneworth and Charles (2013), see Reference 35.

[37] Feldman MP (2014) The character of innovative places: Entrepreneurial strategy, economic development, and prosperity. *Small Business Economics*, 43(1): 9.

5. PUTTING UNIVERSITIES IN THEIR PLACE: THE ORPHIC FRAMEWORK

Keywords: place, ORPHIC Framework, collaboration, policy

5.1 INTRODUCTION

As has been discussed throughout this book, the role of universities in their own regions is undergoing fundamental change. At a global level, the aftermath of the 2008 economic crisis ushered in a decade of austerity in public finances. This led to increased demand for explicit evidence of the returns from or value of public investments, including those from research and higher education (HE). At the same time, international policymakers began to describe the emergence of "grand challenges" (e.g., climate change, ageing, terrorism, sustainability) that are global in their scale and impact, and which orthodoxy suggests cannot be solved by government, academia or business alone. Instead, they require a multidisciplinary and collaborative approach which includes the mobilization of universities and civil society.[1]

There is also pressure from external forces (political and financial) at local and regional levels in motivating universities to become more engaged.[2] This can often be as a result of a particular "crisis driver"[3] (e.g., economic decline) that stimulates universities to make a public commitment to supporting the region. At the same time, local communities and taxpayers facing tough economic conditions might question the value of universities, especially in places where their direct benefits are less apparent (e.g., low levels of local student recruitment, weak levels of graduate retention). This has led to increasing expectations on universities to be proactively engaged in supporting their local area[4] beyond the passive direct and indirect effects of their presence.[5]

More recently, the Covid-19 pandemic has transformed the role of universities in their places, as they have become essential repositories of science, equipment, knowledge and ideas. The pandemic has had wider repercussions for the ability of students and university staff to create true learning environments through physical presence on campuses.

This chapter considers the role of universities in their place. It assesses the challenges for university–place collaboration and drivers of change, before going on to set out a new *ORPHIC Framework* for university and regional contribution. The remainder of this chapter also sets out the test of the framework in practice, by reporting on the results of a worldwide university survey of 100 academics. It ends by highlighting some implications for policymakers.

5.2 CHALLENGES FOR UNIVERSITY–PLACE COLLABORATION

Despite the increasing prominence given to the role of universities in social and economic development, and the range of models available (as set out in chapter 3), research reports and academic studies consistently find that practices are highly fragmented and uncoordinated.[6] There are both internal and external challenges to the effective engagement of universities in local and regional development.[7] Some of these challenges are intrinsic and structural, often driven from a national or even a supra-national level and therefore difficult to overcome at a local scale.

https://doi.org/10.1080/2578711X.2021.1891770

The internal management of universities is in many cases heavily shaped by national funding and regulation of HE, which incentivizes and rewards achievements of esteem indicators for research and (to a lesser extent) teaching excellence (as measured by rankings and league tables) over engagement. Externally, the nature of the place in which the university is located (i.e., economic conditions, and the capacity of the actors in the regional innovation system), can have a profound effect on the contribution even the most well-meaning and motivated universities can make.

5.2.1 Internally derived challenges

Internal tensions in university systems and processes also can act as an impediment to academic engagement;[8] in the internal conflict between achieving esteem indicators for teaching and academic excellence and regional engagement, excellence usually wins.[9] There are also various internal structural factors[10] that, despite pronouncements from senior institutional leaders of their commitment, lead to regional engagement being seen as undermining the excellent, world-class reputation of the university. Individual researchers can have a strong impact on the nature of engagement, and the characteristics of institutions also play an important role, for example, through the size of departments, internal policies and support mechanisms for collaboration.[11]

Incentives, rewards and promotion criteria in universities[12] are important internal mechanisms in stimulating academics to engage with external partners in producing and sharing research. Promotion criteria[13] is probably the most important of these, but one which, to a large extent, still rewards and favours teaching and especially research performance over knowledge transfer or regional engagement activities. This suggests that engaged academics are often acting despite, rather than because of, institutional mechanisms.

While policymakers have sought to motivate universities to become more engaged in local development and innovation through funding and other incentive schemes, these generally lack the scale and significance to sufficiently overcome the internal management issues and tensions.[14] This, in turn, has a substantial impact on academics and their willingness and ability to engage.[15]

5.2.2 Externally derived challenges

The literature and evidence exploring the role of universities in local collaboration points to a range of external factors that limit the potential of (even the most well-meaning and motivated) universities playing a central and valuable role in local and regional development. Two of the most critical of these constraints are the nature of the "place" and the impact of the policy environment.[16]

5.2.2.1 The nature of the place

The extent to which the research being undertaken in universities matches both the local industrial structures and the potential of local firms to apply it is a critical factor in realizing the "promise" of regional economic development policies and the role of universities within them.[17] There is often a mismatch between the research taking place in universities and the innovation requirements of local firms.[18] But even where there might be overlaps between research specialisms and the nature and make-up of the regional economy, insufficient levels of demand-side capacity in the local private sector creates a "wicked problem" for policymakers and regional actors (including universities).

The local impact of university research is severely limited if the business sector has insufficient capacity to absorb and utilize the research outputs (usually referred to as absorptive capacity) of their local universities for knowledge-led growth.[19] This phenomenon is characterized as the "innovation paradox".[20] This refers to the contradiction between a need to invest comparatively greater amounts of public funds in innovation in peripheral regions, but where capacity to absorb these funds and invest in research is lower than in more developed places.

This tends to reinforce the dominance of successful regions and further widen the gap between them and peripheral or lagging ones, as research outputs from the former are absorbed by firms in the latter. This has also been described as the "European paradox",[21] evidenced by weak correlations between research quality and competitiveness, particularly in comparison with the United States. This is attributed to weak external demand-side factors due to suboptimal capacity in local firms as well as insufficient supply-side internal drivers such as incentives and support mechanisms.

A further aggravating factor in peripheral places is one of "institutional thinness",[22] which can be characterized as regions with weak or fragmented industrial clusters and a lack of critical mass of the kinds of organizations (public and private) that support innovation and development.[23] This can lead to an over-dependence on universities to play a dominant role in the local ecosystem, and even an expectation that they fill the gaps created by a paucity of other regional innovation actors.[24] It may further weaken the delivery of their "core" HE missions of teaching and research. This leads to the risk of universities becoming "quasi economic development agencies".[25] This is a role for which they may lack core competencies and indeed cause conflicts of interest, since they may compete for the same funds in which they have a role in governing.

5.2.2.2 Impact of the policy environment

HE policy is often based on national rather than regional needs. Students, particularly at research-intensive, highly ranked universities, tend to be recruited nationally and internationally. Thus, prioritizing teaching and research around narrow, place-specific demands for human and knowledge capital could be seen to limit a university's ability to recruit students and attract research funding.

As discussed above, the incentives and rewards for generating high-quality research do not tend to generate esteem working locally. Indeed, universities with an explicitly local or regional focus might be seen as "second rate" by national policymakers whose concern is achievement against national and international measures of success.[26] A further challenge is that policymakers (and even many commentators) tend to treat universities as relatively homogenous institutions and fail to recognize the significant diversity of

 https://doi.org/10.1080/2578711X.2021.1891770

university types,[27] which is exacerbated by the different policy and place environments in which they operate.[28]

5.3 DEVELOPING A NEW FRAMEWORK FOR COLLABORATION

Policymakers, and even universities themselves, have perhaps fallen into the trap of overestimating the potential contribution of universities in driving local innovation and development, whilst at the same time underplaying the significant impacts of internal tensions and external barriers on their ability and willingness to engage. That is not to suggest they have no direct role as local actors. Rather, we contend that a more realistic, honest understanding of the limitations of universities' contribution as local actors might lead to a more mutually beneficial relationship between them and their places.

As highlighted previously in chapter 3, there have been several attempts in recent years to create conceptual frameworks and models to help universities and policymakers understand the role and contribution of HE to local and regional development. However, these models have failed to fully reflect (or give insufficient attention to) the impact of the regional context (economic, social, political), the policy environment for HE and territorial development, and the diversity of management and leadership structures of universities themselves.

The current policy frameworks for understanding the potential role and contribution of universities to regional development are grounded in a "one size fits all" approach that is often based on specific exemplar cases and empirical evidence from successful regions in the most developed economies (e.g., the UK's "Golden Triangle" of Oxford–Cambridge–London, the MIT Corridor (also known as Route 128), and Silicon Valley, both in the United States) which severely limits their portability as policy instruments to other regions that do not enjoy the same precise conditions of economic success.[29]

This has led to the development of static models that rarely work outside of the immediate context in which they were developed, and therefore risk leading to the design of policies that are not fit for purpose. While there is a growing body of academic and policy or "grey" literature that analyse these issues, so far these have not been translated into a form that can help shape policy.

The overall purpose of this Policy Expo is to develop a new framework to guide policymakers towards a better understanding of the role universities in their regions currently play in regional development, and to identify what actions and policy instruments might best be levered to enhance their potential contribution. This was based on a systematic and comprehensive review of the literature that analysed the problems and challenges in mobilizing universities for regional development, particularly in less developed regions, the learning from which informed the development of a "straw man" framework, articulated in Figure 4.2 in chapter 4.

The framework was tested by exploring the contribution of a higher education institution (HEI) to regional development against a set of regional and institutional characteristics to understand if and, if so, to what extent these impact on the contribution of HEIs. Workshops and seminars with academics, policymakers and practitioners at international conferences were used to develop and road test the key questions needed to build this understanding. This was then developed into an online consultation and call for evidence, which was responded to by 111 Regional Studies Association (RSA) members from institutions in Europe, North America, South America, Africa, Asia and Australia. The analysis of the findings from this consultation informed the "build out" of a new framework, which was presented to academics and policymakers before being finalized.

In terms of the contribution of an HEI, we asked the following questions:

- To what extent are core activities (teaching, research and engagement) aligned to regional need?

- How committed is the institution to supporting regional development? Is it seen as core to its mission or a peripheral activity?

- How are activities that support regional engagement organized? Are they managed and supported in a strategic or an ad-hoc way?

- How does the HEI envision its role in regional development? Does it consider itself a strategic leader or a responsive actor, providing support when asked?

The following regional and institutional characteristics were explored in order to test if and how they impacted on an HEI's contribution to regional development:

- Age and size of the HEI.

- Regional configuration of HE in the region (whether there are few or many HEIs).

- The economic context of the region.

- The policy context for HE and regional development within which the HEI operates.

The breakdown of responses against the options for each classification can be found in Appendix A.

5.4 FINDINGS FROM THE CONSULTATION AND CALL FOR EVIDENCE

5.4.1 Do size and age matter?

HEIs were classified into four age groups based on how long they have been established[30] and four size categories based on the number of enrolled students (Table 5.1).[31]

Respondents from "middle-aged" universities were most likely to see their HEI's teaching as aligned with regional need, possibly reflecting their formation post-1945 when HE policy in many countries had a more spatially focused approach to new institution formation.[32] Academics in young and middle-aged universities felt there was a strong alignment between their institution's research and the needs of the region. While those in older institutions acknowledged an alignment of their research, this was less unequivocal compared with respondents from their younger counterparts. In terms of engagement, there was little

https://doi.org/10.1080/2578711X.2021.1891770

Table 5.1   Age and size classifications of higher education institutes (HEIs)

Age classification	Size classification
Young (< 50 years) Middle aged (50–99 years) Old (100–199 years) Ancient (> 200 years)	Small (< 5000) Mid (5000–19,999) Big (20,000–50,000) Huge (> 50,000)

variation: people in institutions of all ages felt these activities were regionally orientated to a similar extent.

People working in big and huge institutions were considerably more likely (over 50% in both cases) to report their HEI's teaching was totally or largely aligned to regional need compared with just over 30% in the case of small and mid-sized institutions. This may reflect the fact that smaller institutions tend to be more special-ized (e.g., colleges of art) or offer a more limited range of subjects (e.g., business and economics), which may not map particularly to the needs of the regional economy. However, research alignment tended to inversely correlate with size: the smaller the institution, the more likely it was considered that its research aligned with regional need. The alignment of engagement activities was broadly similar across each size group.

Respondents from young and middle-aged universities were more likely to see their HEI as "deeply engaged" and "playing a strategic role" in supporting regional development. While those from older insti-tutions saw them contributing to regional development, this was more peripheral, and their focus was more on their national or international role. This is not particularly surprising as older institutions are more likely to be research intensive and therefore will be oriented towards opportunities for collaborations and fund-ing that will often be outwith the region, as well as being concerned with their position and performance on various league tables.

People in small, mid and big institutions were far more likely than those in huge ones to see their institu-tions as strongly committed to regional development. The bigger the institution, the more likely it was seen to express a commitment to regional development; however, that was not perceived to be matched in practice through delivery.

Academics in the youngest institutions were most likely to describe the organization of regional engage-ment as "strategic and purposeful" and central to everything they do. This might be because HEIs estab-lished in the past 50 years were, in many countries, part of an effort to address HE "cold spots" as well as support economic development in peripheral regions. However, it is interesting that people in young and middle-aged institutions were also more likely than those in older ones to report that while there might be a commitment to regional engagement in principle, this was not always borne out in practice. People from older institutions, especially those universities under 200 years old, were most likely to suggest that regional engagement depended on the motivations of individual academics.

Those based in huge institutions were least likely to describe their HEI's regional engagement as "cen-tral to everything they do". People in small, mid and huge institutions were most likely to say regional engagement was up to an individual's own motivations, while those from big institutions were most likely to report that activities were organized more centrally. This may be because of the likely national/international focus of huge HEIs and lack of central capacity to organize and deliver "third mission" activities in smaller ones (e.g., dedicated teams for regional engagement).

The younger the institution, the more likely their staff were to describe them as a "critical actor" in the region, probably reflecting the mission and founding principles of younger versus older HEIs. The older the institution, the more likely respondents were to see its role as "leading by example" through "spearheading new initiatives".

Those based in younger institutions were also more likely to see it in a passive role, getting involved when asked, but not necessarily playing a proactive role. Some research suggests that in places with multiple HEIs, small and specialist institutions can feel overshadowed by their older, bigger counterparts that tend to be the "go to" place when policymakers want to involve HEIs in regional affairs.

Respondents from small and big institutions were far more likely to see them as critical actors in regional development, while those in huge HEIs are most likely say their role is providing evidence and intelligence for decision-making. Again, this probably reflects the likely national and international orientation of very large HEIs that need to look beyond their region for students and staff, and which intentionally seek national and international reputations.

5.4.2 Does the regional configuration of HE make a difference?

Regional HE configuration was defined in three ways: whether the HEI was the sole HE provider in the region; one of a few (fewer than five); or one of many (five or more). This was to test the assumption that a sole regional HEI was likely to have a closer relationship with its region and to explore whether being one of a few rather than one of many HEIs made a difference.

It would seem that HE configuration had no impact on alignment of teaching to regional need: 80% of respondents said it was totally or largely aligned in their institution regardless of the number of HEIs in the region. Likewise, the responses in terms of engagement were broadly similar, although those from institutions that were one of few in the region were slightly more likely to see it as strongly aligned.

In terms of research, however, there was a very significant difference in responses between those from sole institutions and those who were in one of several HEIs. Those based in sole institutions were around three times more likely to say their research was totally or largely aligned to regional need. This might reflect a purposeful policy of establishing HEIs in what had traditionally been HE "cold spots", whose mandate was often explicitly regional. There was little variation between people in the different configurations in terms of their view of their institution's commitment to regional development, although those in sole HEIs and one of few were slightly more likely to describe them as regionally engaged.

Respondents in sole HEIs were far more likely (over half of all responses) to consider their institution deeply engaged in supporting their region. There was little difference between people based in institutions that

https://doi.org/10.1080/2578711X.2021.1891770

were one of few or one of many in the region. Those in one of multiple institutions were far more likely to say engagement was dependent on the motivation of individuals, with those that were in one of many had the strongest response.

People based in sole HEIs were significantly more likely to say their institution was a critical actor that played a central role in regional decision-making and strategy development than those who were in one of multiple institutions. However, they were also more likely to say their institution did not play a proactive role but got involved when asked. Respondents from HEIs that were one of a few were most likely to describe it as leading by example by spearheading initiatives.

People in institutions who were one of many in the region were most likely to say it made no formal contribution to regional affairs, though only in 10% of cases. No one from a sole institution selected this option.

5.4.3 How significant is the regional economic context?

Four regional context options were defined, based on whether national gross domestic product (GDP) was above or below the Organisation for Economic Co-operation and Development (OECD) average and regional GDP was above or below the national average (Table 5.2).

The regional context seems to have some effect on the alignment of each area of HE activity with regional need. Responses from people based in less developed countries suggest that teaching was more likely to be aligned than in developed countries. In terms of research, alignment was deemed strongest in lagging regions in developed countries and developed regions in less developed countries. It was seen as least aligned in lagging regions in less developed countries, which may be due to lower levels of absorptive capacity in those places.

Similarly, alignment of engagement was considered strongest by people from HEIs in lagging regions in developed countries and developed regions in less developed countries. Weaker alignment in developed regions in developed countries may be attributed to greater "institutional thickness", so less overt demands are placed on HEIs compared with those in less developed regions and countries.

People from HEIs in lagging regions in developed countries and developed regions in less developed countries were most likely to say their institution was deeply engaged in regional development, while responses from the other two classifications were most likely to describe its role as supportive, but with a greater emphasis on their national/international role. Respondents in HEIs in lagging regions in less developed

Table 5.2 Regional economic context

Regional context classification	Definition
Developed region in a developed country	National GDP above the OECD average, regional GDP above the national average
Lagging regional in a developed country	National GDP above the OECD average, regional GDP below the national average
Developed region in a less developed country	National GDP below the OECD average, regional GDP above the national average
Lagging region in a less developed country	National GDP below the OECD average, regional GDP below the national average

Note: GDP, gross domestic product; OECD, Organisation for Economic Co-operation and Development.

countries were most likely to say their HEI was not concerned with regional development, although the number of responses to this was quite small in absolute terms.

Staff in HEIs in lagging regions in less developed countries were most ambivalent about the organization of regional development, with more than 90% saying it was not a big focus in practice or was dependent on individual motivation. People based in institutions in developed regions in developed countries were most likely to say it was not a big focus in practice. Those in lagging regions in developed countries and developed regions in less developed countries were most likely to describe the organization of regional development in their HEI as strategic and purposeful.

Respondents from HEIs in lagging regions in developed countries were much more likely to regard their institution as a proactive actor in regional development, either by playing a central role in strategic leadership or leading by example through spearheading new initiatives. Those from institutions in lagging regions in developing countries were significantly more likely (almost three-quarters of cases) to describe a more passive role, with the institution getting involved when asked to or supplying evidence and data to help with decision-making. Those from HEIs in developed regions in developed countries were also more likely to see their institutions in this role.

5.4.4 What is the effect of the policy context?

There is an underlying assumption that HEIs in places with more devolved powers over regional development will be more likely to be engaged, not least because of the impact of devolution for resource allocation. This factor explored whether or not the HE and regional development policy contexts, specifically the extent to which they are centrally or regionally determined, affected the way HEIs relate to their regions (Table 5.3).

In terms of alignment of teaching to regional need, there was little difference between the various levels of centralized/decentralized policy contexts. While this might at first appear surprising, it probably reflects the fact that HEIs will teach the subjects for which there is demand. For research there was also little variation; in fact, staff from HEIs in places with highly centralized systems were most likely to assess its research as aligned to regional need (although the difference was not very significant). The pattern in terms of engagement was much more distinct, with institutional engagement seen as far more likely to be aligned to regional need the more decentralized the system.

Respondents in HEIs in places where policy and governance are most devolved were most likely to class their institution as deeply committed to supporting regional development, though again there was not a vast difference between the various policy contexts.

Table 5.3 Policy context options

Higher education (HE) policy options	Governance context options
Totally or mostly national determined	Totally centralized/Mainly centralized
Mix of national and regional	Mainly devolved
Mostly or entirely regional	Totally devolved

https://doi.org/10.1080/2578711X.2021.1891770

Those based in HEIs in places where policy is mostly or entirely governed regionally were more likely to see regional engagement as central to, and a core part of, their institution's mission, but again this was not as strong an effect as might have been expected. There was little variation between the systems in considering engagement to be left to individual's motivations, with about a third choosing this option in each group.

In terms of the role of the HEI in regional development, there was again little significant variation with 30% (+/- 3 percentage points) in each policy context ascribing a proactive, leading role for their institution in regional development. One explanation for this might be that places with high levels of regional autonomy may have a denser landscape of agencies and institutions ("institutional thickness") that are focused on regional development, and therefore the pressure for HEIs to actively contribute might not be as acute as in other, institutionally thinner, places.

5.5 INSIGHTS FOR POLICYMAKING

It is important to consider institutional age in regional policymaking. Younger institutions may be overlooked by policymakers in favour of more established, high-profile HEIs.

However, they are more likely to be regionally orientated as older, research-intensive universities are concerned with national and global partnerships. But younger institutions may lack the institutional capacity and resources to support effective engagement.

Policymakers should consider how these activities can be supported and encouraged. They should also be aware that younger institutions, despite having much to offer regional development, may be overlooked in favour of more high-profile, older HEIs. While older HEIs may bring credibility to regional initiatives, they might not be willing to engage unless they can lead them.

Size matters in understanding the role of HEIs in regional development. While intuitively it might be assumed that smaller institutions are more likely than larger ones to orient their teaching to regional need in practice, this is not necessarily the case. Smaller HEIs are more likely to be specialized in specific subject areas (e.g., art, business) that do not necessarily map on to the regional economic structure. Conversely, larger institutions are less likely to align their research to regional need, probably because they need to take a more national and international outlook in recruiting staff and students and may also look beyond the region for sources of research funding.

It is important that policymakers recognize the different roles that HEIs of different sizes play in regional development, and that different mechanisms for engagement might be needed depending on how formally they organize regional activities and how stated commitments translate into practice.

Policymakers must consider the configuration of the HE landscape in their region, but bear in mind that its impacts are not always what might be assumed. HEIs that are one of several or many in the region are just as likely to align their teaching and research to regional need as those that are a sole provider. Likewise, there was little difference in commitment to regional development between the different classifications.

Table. 5.4 *The ORPHIC Framework for University–Regional Collaboration:*

Key questions	Options				Evidence
Orientation of Higher Education Policy					
To what extent is HE policy nationally or regionally focused?	Totally financed and controlled regionally	HE is regionally controlled, but HEIs need to contribute to national targets	HE is centrally controlled, but there is some emphasis on and funding for regional activities	HE entirely centrally controled and spatially blind	National and regional HE policies; Funding settlements and methodologies
Governance of Regional development					
How is regional development governed?	Full autonomy or devolution to the region	Some formal autonomy at the regional level	Some informal autonomy at the regional level	Little/no autonomy	National policies for subnational development; Fiscal powers; Regional governance structures
Characteristics of the Place					
What is the economic character of the region?	Developed region in a developed country	Lagging region in a developed country	Developed region in a less developed country	Lagging region in a less developed country	Regional GDP National GDP
What is the industrial character of the region?	Highly concentrated, thriving	Diverse, thriving	Highly concentrated, declining	Diverse, fragmented	Data on regional businesses by sector and location
How "thick" is the institutional landscape for regional development?	Many public and private actors	Many actors, mostly public	Few actors, mix of public and private	Few actors, mostly public	Regional intelligence; Mapping exercises
Type of HEI					
How big is the HEI?	Small, < 5000 students	Medium, 5000–19,999 students	Large, 20,000–50,000 students	Huge, > 50,000 students	HEI website and annual reports; National HE statistics
How old is the HEI?	Young, < 50 years old	Middle aged, 50–99 years old	Old, 100–199 years old	Ancient, > 200 years old	HEI website; Wikipedia
What is the balance between teaching and research?	Highly research intensive (top 200)	Somewhat research intensive (top 1000)	Mostly teaching focused (some research, not in top 1000)	Entirely teaching focused, no research activity	International league tables
What range of subjects are taught at the HEI?	Full range of arts, humanities, science and engineering	Arts, humanities, and some science and engineering	Art and humanities focused	Technical/vocational focus	HEI prospectus

(Continued)

https://doi.org/10.1080/2578711X.2021.1891770

Table. 5.4 The ORPHIC Framework for University–Regional Collaboration: (Continued)

Key questions	Options				Evidence
What is its position in relation to the regional HE configuration?	Sole HEI in the region	One of few (five or fewer)	One of many (five plus), (one of the biggest)	One of many (five plus), (one of the smallest)	Regional or national data on HEIs
Institutional characteristics					
To what extent is the HEI's research activity oriented to regional need?	Totally	Significantly	Slightly	Not at all	Research strategy; Data on research collaborations; Joint ventures
To what extent is the HEI's teaching activity oriented to the regional need?	Totally	Significantly	Slightly	Not at all	HEI prospectus; Industry involvement in teaching or programme design
To what extent are there incentives or rewards for regional engagement?	Highly rewarded and incentivized	Some rewards and incentives	Few rewards and incentives	No rewards and incentives	Institutional policies; Promotion criteria; Internal funding
Contribution of the HEI					
What role does the HEI play in regional strategies and programmes?	Strategic leader and anchor institution	One of a range of key actors	Manages regional programmes	Reactive, contributes when asked	Institutional strategies; Regional strategies
What is the institutional attitude to participation in regional initiatives?	They are seen as core to its mission and important	One of the things it does	A small part of what it does	No or rare participation in regional initiatives	Initiatives and projects; Non-academic funding success; Regional development offices
What contribution does the HEI make to regional human capital?	Students are mostly recruited from the region and retained after graduation	Students are mostly recruited from outside the region and retained after graduation	Students are mostly recruited from the region and migrate after graduation	Students are mostly recruited from outside the region and migrate after graduation	Data on student region of origin; Data on destinations of graduates

Note: GDP, gross domestic product; HE, higher education; HEI, higher education institutions.

While sole HEIs were much more likely to see themselves playing a central role in regional development, this was not unanimous.

Policymakers should not assume the automatic involvement of HEIs in shaping regional strategies purely on their status as the only one in the region. Where an HEI is one of several in the region, the organization of engagement may be dependent on the motivation of individuals, and therefore may require complex mechanisms to ensure the right people get involved.

The regional context impacts on the way HEIs engage in regional development. Those in lagging regions in developed countries and developed regions in less developed countries are most likely to see their role as central and strategic and align their research accordingly. This might be because of greater demands placed on institutions in these places due to relative institutional thinness, but where there is sufficient absorptive capacity for the outputs of HEIs compared with lagging regions in developing counties.

The stronger alignment of teaching to regional need in less developed countries may reflect an emphasis on the human capital development role of HE in these countries rather than their broader role in regional innovation and development that underpins regional strategy in many developed countries. The relative detachment of HEIs in developed regions in developed countries might be ascribed to institutional thickness in those regions, as well as a tendency towards a more national and international outlook across the economy and its actors more generally.

There can often be an implicit assumption that HEIs in places with greater regional autonomy and control over HE policy will be more orientated to regional development. However, this is not necessarily the case. HEIs in these places will face the same demands as pressures (e.g., student recruitment) as those in places where policy is determined nationally. Furthermore, it is not necessarily the case that centrally controlled policy is spatially blind; HEIs can still be induced and incentivized to play a proactive role in regional development with the right policy design.

A final factor might be the wider institutional context for regional development. Places with devolved systems may have a wide breadth of organizations with a regional remit and therefore the gaps and spaces for HEIs to fill may be more limited than in other, more central, regimes.

5.6 THE ORPHIC FRAMEWORK

Based on extensive consultation and testing of our initial framework with policymakers and HE practitioners, this Policy Expo has developed a "straw man" starting point into a more comprehensive framework which we have called *The ORPHIC Framework*.

"Orphic" means having an import not apparent to the senses or obvious to the intelligence beyond ordinary understanding, reflecting the opaque and sometimes ambiguous nature of the relationships between universities and regions, and is an acronym of the six elements of the framework, namely:

https://doi.org/10.1080/2578711X.2021.1891770

Orientation of Higher Education Policy
Governance of **R**egional development
Characteristics of the **P**lace
Type of **H**EI
Institutional characteristics
Contribution of the HEI

Each element is explored through 16 key questions which were identified as important during the Expo. Four classification options are offered against each for policymakers and their regional HEIs to consider when assessing the potential for cooperation. While some of these are clearly objective (e.g., the size of the HEI), others are more subjective or open to interpretation. To mitigate the latter, the framework requires each response to be evidenced and suggests potential sources of evidence to support the option selected.

Rather than provide a fixed, normative model, our framework offers a flexible approach that can be adjusted to local and institutional conditions, based on a self-assessment process jointly undertaken between key stakeholders. The results of this process can then help universities and their local/regional partners create a tailored and specific approach to contributing to regional development. *The ORPHIC Framework* can help guide policymakers and universities themselves to understand the implications of their *specific* context in determining the potential role and contributions of HE to realizing their regional development goals (Table 5.4).

NOTES

[1] Brennan J, King R and Lebeau Y (2004) *The Role of Universities in the Transformation of Societies: An International Research Project.* Milton Keynes: Centre for Higher Education Research and Information/Association of Commonwealth Universities, UK.

[2] Benneworth, Zeeman N, Pinheiro R and Karlsen J (2017) National higher education policies challenging universities' regional engagement activities. *Ekonomiaz*, 92(2): 112–139.

[3] Benneworth P (2012) The relationship of regional engagement to universities' core purposes: Reflections from engagement efforts with socially excluded communities. In R. Pinheiro and G. A. Jones (eds.), *Universities and Regional Development. A Critical Assessment of Tensions and Contradictions*, pp 199–218. New York: Routledge.

[4] Cochrane A and Williams R (2013) Putting higher education in its place: The socio-political geographies of English universities. *Policy and Politics*, 41(1): 43–58.

[5] Power D and Malmberg A (2008) The contribution of universities to innovation and economic development: In what sense a regional problem? *Cambridge Journal of Regions, Economy and Society*, 1: 233–245.

[6] European Universities Association (2007) *Managing the University Community: Exploring Good Practices.* Brussels: European Universities Association.

[7] Kempton L (2019) Wishful thinking? Towards a more realistic role for universities in regional innovation policy. *European Planning Studies*, 27(11): 2248–2265.

[8] Foray D and Lissoni F (2010) University research and public–private interaction. In BH Hall and N Rosenberg (eds.), *Handbook of Economics of Technical Change*, pp 275–314. North Holland Elsevier.

[9] Marmolejo F and Pukka J (2006) Supporting the contribution of higher education to regional development: Lesson learned from an OECD review of 14 regions through 12 countries. Paper presented at the UNESCO Forum on Higher Education. https://files.eric.ed.gov/fulltext/ED494412.pdf

[10] Benneworth P, Zeeman N, Pinheiro R and Karlsen J (2017) National higher education policies challenging universities' regional engagement activities. *Ekonomiaz*, 92(2): 112–139.

[11] D'Este P and Patel P (2007) University–industry linkages in the UK: What are the factors underlying the variety of interactions with industry? *Research Policy*, 36: 1295–1313.

[12] Lach S and Schankerman M (2008) Incentives and invention in universities. *Rand Journal of Economics*, 39(2): 403–433.

[13] Stanton TK (2008) New times demand a new scholarship: Opportunities and challenges for civic engagement at research universities. *Education, Citizenship and Social Justice*, 3: 19–42.

[14] Kempton L (2016) Institutional challenges and tensions. In J Goddard, E Hazelkorn, L Kempton and P Vallance (eds.), *The Civic University: The Policy and Leadership Challenges*, pp 281–297. Cheltenham: Edward Elgar.

[15] Trippl M, Sinozic T and Lawton Smith H (2015) The role of universities in regional development: Conceptual models and policy institutions in the UK, Sweden and Austria. *European Planning Studies*, 23(9): 1722–1740.

[16] Edwards J, Marinelli, E, Arregui Pabollet, E and Kempton L (2017) *Higher Education for Smart Specialisation— Towards Strategic Partnerships for Innovation* (S3 Policy Brief Series No. 23/2017). Seville: European Commission Joint Research Centre.

[17] Cohen WM and Levinthal D A (1990) Absorptive capacity: A new perspective on learning and innovation. *Administrative Science Quarterly*, 35: 128–152.

[18] Harris R, Fitzpatrick K, Souch C, Brunsdon C, Jarvis C, Keylock C, Orford O, Singleton A and Tate N (2013) *Quantitative Methods in Geography: Making the Connections between Schools, Universities and Employers*. London: Royal Geographical Society with IBG.

[19] Veugelers R and Del Rey E (2014) *The Contribution of Universities to Innovation, (Regional) Growth and Employment* (analytical Report No. 18). Munich: EENEE.

[20] Oughton C, Landabaso M and Morgan K (2002) The regional innovation paradox: Innovation policy and industrial policy. *Journal of Technology Transfer*, 27: 97–110.

[21] European Commission (2007) *Improving Knowledge Transfer between Research Institutions and Industry across Europe: Embracing Open Innovation—Implementing the Lisbon Agenda*. Brussels: European Commission.

[22] Tödtling F and Trippl M (2005) One size fits all? Towards a differentiated regional innovation policy approach. *Research Policy*, 34(8): 1203–1219.

[23] Zukauskaite E, Trippl M and Plechero M (2017) Institutional thickness revisited. *Economic Geography*, 93: 325–345.

[24] Goddard J, Coombes M, Kempton L and Vallance P (2014) Universities as anchor institutions in cities in a turbulent funding environment: Vulnerable institutions and vulnerable places in England. *Cambridge Journal of Regions, Economy and Society*, 7(2): 307–325.

[25]Brown R (2016) Mission impossible? Entrepreneurial universities and peripheral regional innovation systems. *Industry and Innovation*, 23(2): 189–205.

[26]Hazelkorn E (2016) Contemporary debates. Part I: Theorising civic engagement. In J. Goddard, E. Hazelkorn, L. Kempton and P. Vallance (eds.), *The Civic University: The Policy and Leadership Challenges*, pp 34–64. Edward Elgar.

[27]Uyarra E and Flanagan K (2010) From regional systems of innovation to regions as innovation policy spaces. *Environment and Planning C—Governance and Policy*, 28(4): 681–695.

[28]Edwards et al. (2017), see Reference 16; Marlow D, Kempton L and Tewdwr-Jones M (2019) *Inclusive Future Growth in England's Cities and Regions: Realising the Transformational University Dividend*. Newcastle upon Tyne: Newcastle City Futures.[Reference 29 deleted]

[29]Kempton (2019), see Reference 7.

[30]In the case of merged institutions, the age of the oldest of the original institutions was used.

[31]Including under- and postgraduate, full and part-time.

[32]Boucher G, Conway C and Van der Meer E (2003) Tiers of engagement by universities in their region's development. *Regional Studies*, 37: 887–889.

6. RECOMMENDATIONS FOR POLICYMAKERS

Keywords: policy-making, HEIs, regional development

Regional engagement of higher education institutions (HEIs) depends to a large extent on the role an HEI chooses to assume for itself, which is driven by a range of factors, including internal leadership, institution size, age and history. **Policymakers should consider these factors and their impact when designing strategies to involve HEIs in regional development.**

The model of higher education implicit in many approaches to conceptualizing the role of HEIs in regional engagement is often that of a single, large, "full service" anchor institution with a long history of deep ties to its place, and it is rarely the case in practice. Our research demonstrates the reality is often characterized by high levels of heterogeneity of higher education configurations between places. **Policymakers should understand this high level of diversity and avoid duplicating "one size fits all" approaches or models of success from other places.**

In places with multiple HEIs, universities may take on different roles in regional development, depending on their individual characteristics and perceived position compared with the other HEIs in the region. **Policymakers should not therefore treat the sector as a homogenous whole, but rather understand the specificities of its component parts and design policies and programmes that play to the strengths and motivations of individual institutions to maximize their contribution.**

We recommend policymakers use *The ORPHIC Framework* when working with HEIs in their region to understand and map their various roles and contributions. This will help identify gaps and overlaps, which funding programmes can help address by incentivizing HEIs to play new or enhanced roles in line with regional strategies for development.

The importance of the character of the regional context to the contribution HEIs can make to regional development should not be underestimated. **Policymakers should consider these factors in the design of regional programmes and incentivize HEIs to take part in activities that support the development of resilience and adaptive capacity.**

There is no single blueprint for the role of a HEI in regional development over time: it will evolve over time in response to external pressures and internal changes. **Policymakers need a flexible framework to understand the role and contribution HEIs can make to regional development, which should be regularly reviewed and revised in response to changing circumstances.**

Much of the rhetoric on the role of HEIs in regional development is overoptimistic. It ascribes an excessively prominent role for HEIs than evidence would suggest is warranted, and which downplays the significance of the challenges in achieving mutually beneficial outcomes. Ambitious programmes for engaging HEIs in regional development that are not grounded in reality will be at best ineffectual, but may even lead to the widening of disparities between the region and other places. **More modest, but realistic, programmes may prove more effective in the longer term.**

https://doi.org/10.1080/2578711X.2021.1891771

GLOSSARY

Civic university: A kind of place-based university; this concept describes a holistic, institution-wide approach to engagement with society at large. Unlike other models, it pays considerable attention to the internal management and leadership tensions derived from pursuing a "civic" mission. Limitations for regional innovation include a lack of an explicit regional focus—many of the civic university principles are spatially blind—and its description of a normative, idealized model with limited evidence of success in practice.[1]

Engaged university: This model was first introduced by Gunasekera.[2] It moves the role of the university beyond teaching and generation of knowledge to a much wider, developmental one which sees the university collaborating with the wider community (society as well as industry). The focus of the engaged university is on a reciprocal partnership, sharing knowledge and resources for mutual benefit. One of the main limitations of this approach is a lack of verifiable empirical evidence that it makes a positive impact on regional innovation. It also does not take sufficient account of the impact of national and international policy on driving universities' ability or willingness to be "engaged".[3]

Engagement: Activities undertaken by individuals, groups or at institution level in a higher education institution that are not only focused on the teaching of students or academic research. Other terms include outreach, third mission, extension work, community work, service learning, civic or engaged university, etc. It should only refer to activities where at least one participant, partner or beneficiary is from a non-higher education institution sector (business, government, charity, community group, school, cultural or sport activities, etc.).

Entrepreneurial university: This model was first described by Etzkowitz.[4] It describes a "triple helix" of partnership between government, business and the academy where universities complement their traditional research and teaching roles with a "third" mission, namely economic development. The main contribution of the entrepreneurial university to regional innovation is through the commercialization of research by patenting, licensing, etc. Some of the limitations of this model include an underlying assumption of homogeneity of universities and a lack of an explicit regional

https://doi.org/10.1080/2578711X.2021.1891774

focus—a university can implicitly be "entrepreneurial" by working with partners located anywhere. A further critique is that it is based on a US model of drivers and incentives for the commercialization of research which has limited exportability to places with different higher education and innovation policy systems.

Higher education institution (HEI): An HEI or university (public or private) that teaches students to at least first degree (or equivalent) level. May also be involved in postgraduate teaching and research. A university can be defined through its three functions: teaching (the "traditional" main function), research (fundamental to distinguish the universities as institutions) and the "third mission", as a link between the university and society, based on the scientific and technological potential of the university and the specific requests from society. According to the United Nations Educational, Scientific and Cultural Organization (UNESCO),[5] higher education has a mission to educate, train and develop research, contributing to sustainable development and improving society, globally.

Region (place of engagement): A defined geography that can have either formal (e.g., region, state, city-region, federation of local authorities) or informal (e.g., regional associations) structures of governance between national central/federal government and local administration (e.g., county, local authority, city, municipality, etc.) levels. The region/local of impact could be distinct depending on the function that is under analysis.

Regional innovation system (RIS): This approach is described by Cooke et al.[6] The approach to regional innovation describes universities playing a central role both as knowledge generators and as a connector between public and private actors in the region. Therefore, this puts universities at the heart of regional innovation and not just as one of several actors, but as a key driving force. Some of the limitations of this approach include a neglect of the cultural and social aspects of regional development, and the role that civil society could play.[7]

Smart Specialisation Strategy (RIS3): Smart Specialisation ascribes a key role to universities as actors in their local innovation ecosystems, connecting global and local knowledge domains. Working together with the public sector, business and other social partners could provide exiting opportunities for universities to broaden their role locally and not only contribute to their "engagement" mission, but also enhance the impact of their teaching and research, something governments and funding bodies are increasingly looking for.[8]

System-based university: This is defined by the higher education institution's embeddedness within a territorial innovation system, and its network relationships with other local innovation actors in the private and public sectors (chapter 3). This model is aligned with the regional innovation system approach for which the universities are the main actors of a region's knowledge infrastructure.[9] A regional innovation system implies the connection between the territorial agents as well as the ability to promote innovation systematically. Therefore, knowledge occurs in the context of application and higher education institutions are the main contributors to the solution of societal problems.

https://doi.org/10.1080/2578711X.2021.1891774

Triple helix: A conceptual model of innovation and economic development based on dynamic university–industry–government relations.[10] It was introduced in the mid-1990s by Loet Leydesdorff and Henry Etzkowitz.[11] The triple helix has become influential in policy as well as academic debates at an international level, in part through the activities of the Triple Helix Association. Its development is closely tied to the model of an entrepreneurial university (see above).

NOTES

[1] Adapted from Kempton L (2018) Solução milagrosa ou o ouro dos tolos? O papel das universidades nos sistemas regionais de inovação. In M Serra, C Rolim and AP Bastos (eds.), *Universidades e Desenvolvimento Regional—as bases para a inovação competitiva*. Rio de Janeiro: Ideia D, at 60–61.
[2] Gunasekara C (2004) The regional role of universities in technology transfer and economic development. *British Academy of Management Conference*, 30 August - 1 September, St Andrews, Scotland.
[3] Kempton (2018), p. 60, see Reference 1.
[4] Etzkowitz H (1983) Entrepreneurial scientists and entrepreneurial universities in American academic science. *Minerva*, 21(2–3): 198–233.
[5] UNESCO (1998); World Conference on Higher Education, Paris, October. Avalaible at: https://www.iau-hesd.net/sites/default/files/documents/1998_-_higher_education_in_the_twenty-first_century_vision_and_action_fr.pdf Accessed in May 2020.
[6] Cooke P, Heidenreich M and Braczyk H (2004) Regional Innovation systems: an evolutionary approach. In: P Cooke, M Heidenreich and H-J Braczyk (eds.), *Regional Innovation Systems: The Role of Governance in a Globalized World*, pp 1–18. London: Routledge.
[7] Kempton (2018), pp 59–60, see Reference 1.
[8] Kempton L, Goddard J, Edwards J, Hegyi F B and Elena-Pérez S (2014) *Universities and Smart Specialisation*. JRC Technical Reports. S3 Policy Brief Series N. 03/2013. Luxembourg: Publications Office of the European Union. doi: 10.2791/52851.
[9] Uyarra E (2010) Conceptualizing the regional roles of universities, implications and contradictions. *European Planning Studies*, 18(8): 1227–1246; Trippl M, Sinozic T and Lawton Smith H (2015) The role of universities in regional development: Conceptual models and policy institutions in the UK, Sweden and Austria. *European Planning Studies*, 23(9): 1722–1740.
[10] Etzkowitz H (2008) *The Triple Helix: University–Industry–Government Innovation in Action*. London: Routledge.
[11] Leydesdorff L and Etzkowitz H (1998). The Triple Helix as a model for innovation studies, *Science and Public Policy*, 25(3): 95–203, https://doi.org/10.1093/spp/25.3.195.

APPENDIX A: RESPONSES TO THE SURVEY QUESTIONNAIRE

Age	%	Size	%	Configuration	%	Context[a]	%	Higher education policy	%	Regional policy	%
Young	29.1%	Small	32.1%	Sole	13.8%	DR-DC	42.3%	Centralized	58.6%	Centralized	15.3%
Middle	22.7%	Medium	26.6%	One of few	43.1%	LR-LC	26.1%	Mix	22.5%	Mainly centralized	46.8%
Old	35.5%	Big	31.2%	One of many	43.1%	DR-LDC	17.1%	Devolved	13.5%	Some devolution	23.4%
Ancient	10.0%	Huge	10.1%			LR-LDC	10.8%			Devolved	5.4%
Don't know/other	2.7%	Don't know/other	-	Don't know/other	-	Don't know/other	3.6%	Don't know/other	5.4%	Don't know/other	10.0%

Note: [a]DC, developed country; DR, developed region; and LR, lagging region.

https://doi.org/10.1080/2578711X.2021.1891776

REGIONAL STUDIES POLICY IMPACT BOOKS

The Regional Studies Policy Impact books are series of "Expo" publications from the Regional Studies Association. The books in this series are commissioned to address topical policy questions of contemporary importance to all communities engaged in regional and urban studies issues. The term "Expo" is taken to mean "a comprehensive description and meaning of an idea or theory". The publication style uses clear and coherent narrative addressing evidence for different policy and theoretical positions. Each topic is broad in scope, achieving global reach and relevance wherever possible. There is a consistent focus on the impact of policy research both in terms its reach to policy, academic and practitioner communities and also in its significance, to show how evidence can inform policy change within regional and urban studies.

The Belt and Road Initiative as epochal regionalisation

Xiangming Chen with Julie Tian Miao and Xue Li (2020)

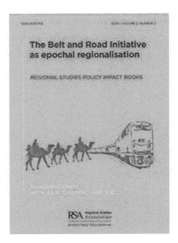

The Belt and Road Initiative (BRI), launched by China in 2013, carries and projects powerful regional dimensions and transformations, with short- and long-term global, national and local consequences. The BRI's regional significance lies in its designation and creation of several cross-border corridors that originate from inside China and extend out into its neighbouring countries, and those farther afield in Asia, Africa and Europe. Through driving and facilitating new trade and infrastructure connections along and beyond these corridors, the BRI has begun to reshape the master processes of globalisation, urbanisation and development by affecting the economic, social and spatial fortunes of many countries and cities.

This book serves two purposes. First, through a new framework and three case studies, it examines the BRI's impacts on globalisation, urbanisation and development via the China-Europe Freight Train, the paired construction of a new city and railway across the China-Laos borderland and the port-park-city development corridor between Djibouti and Ethiopia. Second, the comparative analysis and evidence guide the book to advance policy recommendations for targeted stakeholders that can potentially turn the BRI into a global public good with greater benefits and fewer risks.

Every place matters: towards effective place-based policy

By Andrew Beer, Fiona McKenzie, Jiří Blažek, Markku Sotarauta & Sarah Ayres (2020)

Across the globe policy makers implement, and academics teach and undertake research upon, place-based policy. But what is place-based policy, what does it aspire to achieve, what are the benefits of place-based approaches relative to other forms of policy, and what are the key determinants of success for this type of government intervention? This Policy Expo explores the differing perspectives on place-based policy and maps out the essential components of effective and impactful actions by government at the scale of individual places.

Revitalising Lagging Regions: Smart Specialisation and Industry 4.0

Edited By Mariachiara Barzotto, Carlo Corradini, Felicia M Fai, Sandrine Labory & Philip R Tomlinson (2019)

This Expo book brings together leading academic and policymaker experts to reflect on the significant challenges faced by lagging regions in participating in the European Union's Research and Innovation Strategies for Smart Specialisation (RIS3) programme. In doing so, the book offers a set of new policy recommendations on the design and implementation of appropriate Smart Specialisation Strategies (S3) in lagging regions, which may enable them to benefit from the opportunities of digitalisation and Industry 4.0 (I4.0).

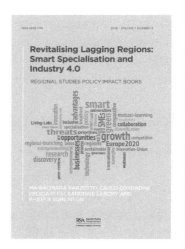

Towards Cohesion Policy 4.0: Structural Transformation and Inclusive Growth

By John Bachtler, Joaquim Oliveira Martins, Peter Wostner and Piotr Zuber (2019)

In the context of the debate on the future of Europe, this book makes the case for a new approach to structural transformation, growth and cohesion in the EU. It explores both the opportunities and challenges from globalisation and technological change, the widening differences in productivity between leading and lagging regions, and the need for a new policy framework capable of delivering inclusive growth.